Paragraph

A Journal of Modern Critical Theor.

Volume 37, Number 2, July 2014

Francophone Communities Past and Present

Edited by Charles Forsdick, Mairéad Hanrahan and Martin Munro

Contents

This publication is available as a book (ISBN: 9780748692491) or
as a single issue or part of a subscription to *Paragraph*, Volume 37
(ISSN: 0264-8334). Please visit www.euppublishing.com/para for
more information.

Paragraph is indexed in the Arts & Humanities Citation Index and
Current Contents/Arts & Humanities

Introduction: Francophone Communities Past and Present

CHARLES FORSDICK, MAIRÉAD HANRAHAN AND MARTIN MUNRO

'Francophone Postcolonial Theory', the Special Issue of *Paragraph* edited in 2001 by Celia Britton and Michael Syrotinski, played a determining role in shaping the research field it sought to map. Much has changed in the decade since then, both in Francophone postcolonial criticism and in the specific context of Caribbean literature and thought. From at least the late 1980s, the greater part of Francophone Caribbean criticism tended to deal primarily with the French Departments of Martinique, Guadeloupe and, to a lesser extent, Guyane. The considerable intellectual energy that underpinned the great literary and cultural movements from those regions — *Négritude, Antillanité* and *Créolité* — drew the majority of critical attention from Francophone Caribbeanists. Haiti, by contrast, was relatively ignored and deemed to be somewhat on the margins of the intellectual movements that seemed to be arranged teleologically, or even dialectically, marking a specific point in a trajectory that appeared to lead irresistibly to a future, or futures, characterized by infinite reinventions of Francophone Caribbean identities, and a general openness to the ever-creolizing world — 'le monde se créolise' in Glissant's well-known phrase.[1] Remarkably, then, the last ten years or so have seen an almost complete reversal in this Antillean-Haitian dynamic. Since at least 2004, the year of the bicentenary of Haitian independence and of the controversial departure of President Jean-Bertrand Aristide, there has been a decided 'Haitian turn' in Francophone Caribbean studies, a rush of scholars from multiple disciplines taking a new interest in Haiti, and a turn among many more established Caribbeanists towards Haiti. The earthquake of 2010

Paragraph 37.2 (2014): 155–159
DOI: 10.3366/para.2014.0118
© Edinburgh University Press
www.euppublishing.com/para

precipitated a further surge in scholarly interest in Haiti, and at the same time has led to a great proliferation of works — articles, monographs, edited volumes, special issues of journals — on themes as diverse as Haitian literature, politics, history, religion and music.[2]

The same period has been marked by the deaths of the two great figureheads of French Antillean writing — Aimé Césaire in 2008, and Édouard Glissant in 2011. While the legacy of both lives on in the remarkable bodies of work, which will certainly continue to attract and inspire intellectual engagement, the physical deaths of two such influential figures have each left a considerable void in French Caribbean writing. The last ten years or so in Antillean writing have to some extent been marked by endings — the physical passings of Césaire and Glissant, which marked the end of the intellectual eras they created and embodied, but also the slow but apparently inevitable movement of their most obvious heirs, the Creolists, into various forms of creative and conceptual dead-ends. Criticized from its beginnings for, among other things, its apparent essentialism, its overt masculinism, and its reduction of Caribbean 'authenticity' to a set of stock, folkloric figures, *Créolité* appears to have reached something of an impasse, which itself marks the apparent end of the 'Holy Trinity' of *Négritude-Antillanité-Créolité* that has shaped the last seventy years or so of French Caribbean intellectualism.

Ever susceptible to broader political, economic and cultural shifts, the Caribbean has felt directly the effects of the various global crises that have shaped the past fifteen years — wars, environmental disasters, migrations, economic disasters — so that the prevailing understandings of the Caribbean present tend to cast it in terms of tragedy, of living still in an unfinished, catastrophic history, far removed from the decidedly utopian, open-ended conceptions of time and cultural renewal that characterized some of the major critical and theoretical writings of the 1980s and 1990s. At the same time, an increased focus on the legacies of Atlantic slavery — associated with commemorations such as the sesquicentenary of the second abolition of slavery in the French empire as well as with the key legislation of the *loi Taubira* — has underlined key aspects of that unfinished past specific to the Caribbean but also created connexions to other zones such as the Indian Ocean.

The sense of a tragic, dystopian Caribbean present is suggested in the visual art project undertaken in 2011 by the journal *Small Axe*, entitled 'The Visual Life of Catastrophic History'. The project is a response to the coming to prominence of the theme of catastrophe in a number of domains of critical thought and artistic practice. The reasons offered for this coming to prominence are largely predictable: the 'wars without end' unleashed by 'emperor-like sovereigns'; the personal and social effects of systemic financial collapse; the destructive force of natural events such as tsunamis, hurricanes and earthquakes; and the 'terrible spectacle' of the most vulnerable people fleeing in fear 'the total power of men and gods'.[3] Together, these calamities create the 'pervasive haunting sense' that we are living in 'a perpetual state of emergency, not only in the very midst of seemingly uncontrollable disaster but also in a constant expectation of disaster' (133). And, in stark contrast to the Romantic vision of history and time critiqued by the *Small Axe* editor David Scott in his influential *Conscripts of Modernity*,[4] such a scene of catastrophe is marked by a temporal block, the effect of which is to make the future almost impossible to envision in terms other than as a continued disaster. This is what the project statement means when it refers to the 'paralyzing *futurelessness* of catastrophe' (134).

Within this global scenario of disaster, the Caribbean is 'a measureless scene of catastrophe', a site particularly prone and susceptible to calamities, to various natural disasters and social and political atrocities (134). The statement further argues that the Caribbean was '*inaugurated* in catastrophe': the Spanish colonial enterprise that led to the swift extermination of native peoples. Subsequent Caribbean history is conceived of in the statement as a series of catastrophes that range from the capture, transportation and enslavement of Africans to the indentureship of Chinese and East Indians. 'In fundamental ways', the statement proposes, 'the Caribbean has never overcome this founding colonial catastrophe', the reverberations of which have shaped to a considerable extent the postcolonial history of the region to the present day in the form of economies driven by 'external imperatives', societies structured with 'tiny rapacious elites' at one end and 'impoverished masses' at the other, and 'cynical, unresponsive governments given to authoritarian rule and corruption' (134).

The tragic, even apocalyptic tenor of the Caribbean present was perhaps most strikingly manifested in the Haitian earthquake of 2010, an event that further complicates the notions of time and history that Scott writes of: did the earthquake mark the end of an historical period and as such liberate the present and the future from the tragic past, or is it just one further instance in an unendingly catastrophic historical movement, itself made inevitable by history and its legacies of twisted social relations, environmental degradation, and economic marginalization?

Criticism is of course itself subject to shifts, generational movements that are responses to changing intellectual, social, political and historical climates. In Scott's terms, generations are formed when an otherwise disparate group of individuals assumes a collective identity 'by virtue of their location in relation to *eventful* collective experience, such as wars, riots, revolutions, natural catastrophes, and the like'.[5] Generations and communities of critics are no doubt formed also in relation to key works, authors and movements, as well as the factors that Scott describes. This new issue of *Paragraph* therefore marks something of a generational shift from the 2001 issue edited by Celia Britton and Michael Syrotinski. To be sure, a number of the authors of that first issue are also published here, but they are joined by and their works past and present put into dialogue with a newer generation of Caribbeanists in a dynamic that suggests an ongoing process of critical renewal.

This issue therefore brings together new and original work by some of the leading scholars in those fields. The contributions draw on material from different historical moments, ranging from the nineteenth century to the contemporary period, and explore questions of literature, culture, society and thought from across the Francophone Caribbean and beyond. As the collection originates in a conference held in honour of Celia Britton in University College London in June 2011, many of the articles focus on the spaces and issues in relation to which her work proved most influential. Several — particularly the articles by Charles Forsdick, Kate Hodgson, and Martin Munro — engage directly with her work and the key concepts, notably community, that it has explored. Others extend her exploration of contemporary Caribbean authors (Lorna Milne on Chamoiseau and Pineau, Eva Sansavior on Condé, Eli Park Sorensen on Phillips). Still others demonstrate vividly how the questions that underpinned her research on the Caribbean over the past two decades have proved not only relevant but immensely fruitful in relation to the wider postcolonial context (Michael Syrotinski on postcolonial thought and contemporary Francophone African Literature, Maeve McCusker on race and whiteness, Mary Gallagher on academic communities). Signalling some of the new and emerging directions in Caribbean studies and postcolonial studies, this volume provides an opportunity to identify the most pressing questions currently at stake in our understanding of the diverse modes and forms through which

Francophone communities relate and have related within themselves, to each other and to the wider world.

NOTES

1 Édouard Glissant, *Introduction à une poétique du Divers* (Paris: Gallimard, 1996), 15–16.

2 For critical surveys of recent work on Haiti, see: Celucien L. Joseph, ' "The Haitian Turn": An Appraisal of Recent Literary and Historiographical Works on the Haitian Revolution', *Journal of Pan-African Studies* 5 (2012), 37–55; Charles Fordick, 'After the Earthquake: Some Reflections on Recent Scholarship', *Bulletin of Francophone Postcolonial Studies* 4:2 (2013), 2–8; Philippe Girard, 'The Haitian Revolution, History's New Frontier: State of the Scholarship and Archival Sources', *Slavery and Abolition* 34:1 (2013), 485–507; Martin Munro, 'Whose and Which Haiti? Western Intellectuals and the Aristide Question', *Paragraph* 36:3 (2013), 408–24; Matthew J. Smith, 'Haiti from the Outside In: A Review of Recent Literature', *Radical History Review* 115 (2013), 203–11.

3 'The Visual Life of Catastrophic History: A Small Axe Project Statement', *Small Axe* 34 (2011), 133–6 (133); subsequent references in the text.

4 David Scott, *Conscripts of Modernity: The Tragedy of Colonial Enlightenment* (Durham, NC: Duke University Press, 2004).

5 David Scott, *Omens of Adversity: Tragedy, Time, Memory, Justice* (Durham, NC: Duke University Press, 2014), 72.

From the 'Aesthetics of Diversity' to the 'Poetics of Relating': Segalen, Glissant and the Genealogies of Francophone Postcolonial Thought

CHARLES FORSDICK

Abstract:
The article explores the 'significant missed rendezvous' and posthumous critical dialogue between Victor Segalen (1878–1919) and Édouard Glissant (1928–2011). It studies the ways in which the Martinican novelist, poet and theorist identified Segalen as a catalytic presence in his thought and as one of his privileged, lifelong interlocutors. The study tracks the role of Segalen's work in the steady emergence and elaboration of Glissant's thought, but also analyses the place of Glissant's readings in the progressive reassessment of Segalen's own writings (and particularly in their recent recontextualization in a postcolonial frame). The article contributes to reflections on the formation of communities of thought in which intellectuals from different moments and different ideological niches — in this case colonial and postcolonial — are drawn into dialogue in ways that appear achronological. Segalen and Glissant are presented as part of a wider community of French-language writers, linked with 'relational' ties, whose engagements with questions of contact and cultural diversity overlap, intersect and ultimately interact.

Keywords: Victor Segalen, Édouard Glissant, exoticism, Diversity, Relation, postcolonialism, Francophone thought

> Diversity is in decline. Therein lies the great earthly threat. It is therefore against this decay that we must fight, fight amongst ourselves — perhaps die with beauty.[1]

Paragraph 37.2 (2014): 160–177
DOI: 10.3366/para.2014.0119

Diversity is not the melting-pot, the pulp, the mish-mash, etc. Diversity is differences that encounter each other, adjust to each other, oppose each other, agree with each other and produce the unpredictable. Standardization is certainly a danger, but the very idea of the Tout-Monde helps to combat this danger.[2]

Towards the end of his life, Jorge Luis Borges is reported to have commented, to an unidentified 'French poet friend':

The French talk about Valéry and even the preposterous Péguy with adoration — don't they know that in Victor Segalen they have one of the most intelligent writers of our age, perhaps the only one to have made a fresh synthesis of Western and Eastern aesthetics and philosophy? (...) [D]o not live another month before you have read the entire oeuvre. (...) You can read Segalen in less than a month, but it might take you the rest of your life to begin to understand him.[3]

It is this idea of a struggle with the Segalenian text — 'tak[ing] the rest of your life to begin to understand' — that this article adopts as its point of departure. The aim is to explore a specific example of what James Clifford, in the context of the posthumous engagement of the Breton writer and traveller Segalen with the painter Paul Gauguin, has called a 'significant missed rendezvous'.[4] The case in this study relates to the similarly skewed and posthumous dialogue between Segalen (1878–1919) and Édouard Glissant (1928–2011) — although on this occasion, it is the Breton author and theorist of diversity himself whose premature death prevented any actual meeting between the two men, and it is the Martinican novelist, poet and theorist who identified Segalen as a catalytic presence in his thought and as one of his privileged, lifelong interlocutors. The article considers the role of Segalen's work in the steady emergence and elaboration both of Glissant's thought and of the terminology that has increasingly served as a vehicle for it in the postcolonial field. The study also explores the place of Glissant's readings in the progressive reassessment of Segalen's own writings, and particularly in their recent recontextualization in a postcolonial frame.

As such, what follows provides a reflection on the formation of communities of thought in which intellectuals from different moments and different ideological niches — in this case distinctively (and not unproblematically) colonial and postcolonial — are drawn into dialogue in ways that appear achronological. For, as products of very different sets of geographical, historical and political circumstances, and as writers associated respectively with colonial and postcolonial literature and thought, Segalen and Glissant nevertheless may be seen to belong to an eclectic community of 'Francophone postcolonial intellectuals'.[5] They can also be identified as part of a wider community of French-language writers — including figures such as Montesquieu — whose relationship to otherness is characterized by an ability, in Sidi Omar Azeroual's terms, to 'adopter une stratégie de *discours avec* au lieu d'instaurer un *discours sur*'[6] (adopt a strategy of *discoursing with* instead of establishing a *discourse about*). The article falls into two main sections, the first of which explores the ways Segalen and Glissant's reflections on questions of contact and cultural diversity overlap, intersect and ultimately interact; the second section draws on the work of Celia Britton, the first to comment in detail on the links between Glissant and postcolonial theory, in order to focus more specifically on the ways in which this interaction contributes in particular to the development of thought in the postcolonial field.

Segalen and Glissant: Critical Consumption and Entangled Thinking

Victor Segalen and Édouard Glissant — through their attention, in very different contexts and at very different historical moments, to intercultural dynamics and the persistence of diversity — were both 'confronted with the tragic degradation of the human'.[7] Together, their work has generated (or, at the least, been deployed to illuminate) some of the key terms and concepts that have shaped postcolonial studies and (perhaps more importantly) have delineated the French and Francophone contours of a field understood, initially at least, as a primarily Anglophone one. In this context, the relationship between the pair is not to be understood, as Jean-Louis Cornille has implied it might be, as one of unidirectional plagiarism by a living author of a dead one.[8] Instead, it constitutes a more complex process of mutual illumination (what Cornille himself suggests might be seen as 'métissage littéraire' (MC, 173) (literary hybridization)) whereby the anti-colonial and postcolonial writer Glissant elaborates his own thinking iteratively via the detour of reading and re-reading an *œuvre* that emerged from the context of high imperialism. In this process of elaboration of new thinking around Segalen's work, Glissant contributes to the discernment of meaning in a largely forgotten body of writing largely incomprehensible to those contemporary to its production. Kenneth White has suggested that the disruptive potential of Segalen's work resides in 'l'actualité de l'inactualité'[9] (the topicality of the lack of topicality) that it reveals, and it is, in large part, through Glissant's evolving and heuristic engagement with texts such as *Stèles* and the *Essai sur l'exotisme* that this early twentieth-century reflection on exoticism and cultural diversity has found a new readership in the context of decolonization and, more recently, of contemporary globalization and postcoloniality.

In his eulogy for Édouard Glissant delivered at l'Anse Caffard and published in February 2011, Patrick Chamoiseau identified Segalen — dubbed 'ce bon Segalen qui déchiffre l'errance' (good Segalen who deciphered wandering) — as one of the cluster of key artists and thinkers with whom the recently deceased Martinican intellectual had engaged throughout his whole adult life.[10] Segalen is associated in Chamoiseau's designation with a key concept in Glissant's work, that of 'wandering' — and, more specifically, with the 'wanderer'. This is a figure described by Celia Britton in *Édouard Glissant and Postcolonial Theory* as one who 'explores the world, aspires to know it in its totality, but realizes that he never will', and also for whom this ultimate unknowability reveals the 'infinitely open-ended, uncontainable aspect of Relation'.[11] As Chamoiseau suggests, Segalen serves as a constant point of reference in Glissant's work. This process began with the early engagement in the 1950s, when Glissant produced a review essay originally and enthusiastically entitled 'Segalen, Segalen!' in *Les Lettres nouvelles* (subsequently included in *L'Intention poétique*).[12] At the same time, he also factored lexical indications of Segalenian influence into his early poetry (*Le Sang rivé* contains references, for instance, to 'Océanie' and 'sampan'; critics have detected resonances between *Stèles* and *Les Indes*).[13] This engagement continued then through to the work of his final years, the period now associated with the 'late Glissant', in whose work references to the theorist and poet of exoticism continued to be prominent: Segalen is present in the collected interviews with Alexandre Leupin and Lise Gauvin that appeared with Gallimard (in 2008 and 2010 respectively);[14] *Quand les murs tombent*, the 2007 pamphlet written with Chamoiseau as a critique of the Ministry of National Identity, acts as another stage in a dialogue with Segalenian notions of identity, diversity and the aesthetics of difference;[15] and finally, extracts from Segalen's *Equipée* and *Stèles* that featured in *La Terre, le feu, l'eau et les vents*, subtitled as an *anthologie de la poésie du Tout-Monde*, a collection that appeared shortly before Glissant's death in 2010.[16]

The persistent presence of Segalen in Glissant's work and thought across a period of over five decades illustrates the extent to which the early twentieth-century writer has provided, throughout the century following his death in 1919, an illuminating case study in intellectual and literary afterlives and in their implications for the construction of communities of thought. At his premature death at the age of forty-one, Segalen, the poet, novelist, essayist, travel writer and naval doctor, had published only three texts: the Tahitian ethnographic novel narrating the 'fatal impact' of Western incursions in the Pacific, *Les Immémoriaux* (1907); and two collections of prose poems inspired by Chinese cultural models, *Stèles* (1912) and *Peintures* (1916). Other keys works — such as the proto-New Novel *René Leys*, and the unfinished *Essai sur l'exotisme* — remained in manuscript, fragments of a body of work of which large parts still remain unpublished. Segalen's precocious modernity was for several decades obscured and largely ignored as a result of an interpretation that over-privileged its orientalizing, post-Symbolist dimensions. The Belgian surrealist poet Norge describes the discovery of remaindered copies of the poet's work on the stalls of *bouquinistes* along the Parisian *quais* in the 1930s,[17] and it took until the end of the last century — and most notably until the publication of a largely provisional edition in two volumes of *œuvres complètes* by Laffont in the 'Bouquins' series in 1995 and the inclusion of Segalen on the *agrégration* programme in 1999 — for widespread critical attention to be paid.[18] The intervening decades reveal nevertheless a striking process of excavation and engagement, in which Glissant was one of a number of eminent yet diverse readers who grappled with what Timothy Billings and Christopher Bush have dubbed (in their excellent English-language translation of *Stèles*) the 'readerly challenges' of Segalen's work.[19] These prominent interpreters constitute a suitably diverse network, including Giorgio Agamben, Jean Baudrillard, James Clifford, Pierre Jean Jouve, Tzvetan Todorov, Michael Gilsenan, Patrick Chamoiseau and Kenneth White. In the vanguard of this select group of readers were, however, two key Francophone postcolonial authors and critics, Abdelkebir Khatibi and Glissant himself, both of whom — in the upheaval of decolonization in the 1950s — discovered in Segalen's work tools for the analysis of their own respective situations and of the immediate contexts of global transformation of which these formed a part.

Connexions between Khatibi and Glissant — beyond their evident status as Francophone postcolonial intellectuals, belonging to a generation whose thought was shaped by anti-colonial struggle and the challenges of decolonization — are not immediately apparent. Both, however, used their work to explore the complex relationship to the French language of the postcolonial writer operating in French; both also engaged closely with contemporary French philosophy and thought, proposing what might be seen in retrospect as the progressive 'postcolonialization' of intellectual culture emerging from the metropolitan centre; finally, as Silke Segler-Messner notes, both discerned in Segalen the roots of another kind of poetics, identifying in the process 'the fin-de-siècle *exote* as the initiator of an alternative form of literary description, which explores spaces and places, and is concerned with the interstitial and a third dimension of the other'.[20] In this context, the actively critical consumption and reframing of Segalen by Glissant and Khatibi may be seen as a form of intellectual cannibalism, with such an analysis echoing reflections by the Brazilian modernist movement in the 1920s on cultural anthropophagy — and the ways in which imported cultural influences must be absorbed, digested and critically reconfigured in terms of the local context of its consumption.[21] Khatibi provides a clear frame in which to understand the ways other postcolonial intellectuals such as Glissant engaged with Segalen. In an interview with Jean Scemla in 1984, Khatibi describes, for instance, his experience of reading Segalen along such lines: 'I think we need to distance ourselves from Segalen whilst consuming him, i.e. whilst absorbing him magically.'[22] The Moroccan sociologist and author had described, in *La Mémoire tatouée* (1971), his introduction to Segalen's Polynesian works three decades earlier by a literature teacher at the *lycée français* in Casablanca in the 1950s: 'When he explained Segalen by underlining the death of cultures, I know that he was giving me weapons.'[23] Khatibi appears to refer here to *Les Immémoriaux*, a text that was reissued in 1955 by Jean Malaurie in Plon's 'Terre humaine' series, alongside Lévi-Strauss's *Tristes tropiques* (a work that similarly outlines the erosion of cultural distinctiveness and the entropic imposition of a global monoculture). It was his exploration of the same kinds of questions that drew Glissant to Segalen's work as — during his first stay in France — he sought to understand the implications of the persistently colonial, transatlantic axes that tied Martinique to contemporary France.

Glissant initially discovered Segalen in the 1955 'Club du Meilleur Livre' edition of *Stèles, Peintures, Equipée*, his review of which in *Les Lettres nouvelles* is mentioned above. Although produced in a limited edition of 5,000, this edition provided for the first time access to Segalen's key Chinese texts, and also, perhaps more importantly, included extensive extracts from the *Notes sur l'exotisme*, the fragmented manuscript of the essay on exoticism that had previously only appeared in a heavily abridged form several years earlier in the *Mercure de France*.[24] Jean-Louis Cornille has captured the impact of this textual encounter — occurring, almost certainly, 'without any prior knowledge' — on the young Glissant: 'to judge by the lasting impact that this work had on him, it must have been a real revelation to read it out of the blue, while he was in the midst of this own writing' (MC, 176); and Jean-Pol Madou similarly describes an 'overwhelming revelation'.[25] The initial discovery of Segalen outlined not least for Glissant an investigative literary form, based on the essay, that he would deploy for much of the rest of his career, most notably in the cycle of texts subtitled 'poétique'. This is a provisional, evolving genre in Glissant's work, described in the interviews with Lise Gauvin as 'a tool of discovery' that permitted its author to 'delve into a matter' (*ELG*, 74); as Jean-Pol Madou comments, the intellectual practices encapsulated in the Segalenian *équipée* are closely linked to those of the Glissantian *drive* (*LGS*, 73),[26] but at the same time, Glissant moves beyond form to discover in Segalen key terms and concepts that he would use as foils to develop his own emerging understanding of cultural distinctiveness and diversity. Traces of this engagement with Segalen are already evident in *Soleil de la conscience* in 1956, not least in the anti-entropic, anti-colonial observation that: 'there will be no culture without all cultures, no other civilization that can be the metropolis of others'.[27] Such a claim — a decade after departmentalization in the French Caribbean — was firmly grounded in a clear understanding of the subjectivity of the colonized and in a clear reassertion of the relativity and the bilateral nature of the exotic gaze as expressed in *L'Intention poétique*: 'You say overseas (we have said it with you), but you are also soon overseas' (*IP*, 21). Echoing the sense of a pivotal reversal of the gaze encapsulated in the observation in the *Essai sur l'exotisme* ('the familiar "tu" will dominate') (*EE*, 17), Glissant appears to draw from Segalen a precociously early understanding of exoticism that presents the concept not reductively or schematically (that is, not as 'entirely negative or entirely exhilarating' (*ELG*, 17)), but as variable and even volatile. Central to this engagement with Segalen is this recognition that terms evolve and that concepts travel, with the result that there is a meticulous job of contextualization required to understand how a word such as 'le Divers' migrates from an early twentieth-century use in a text such as the *Essai sur l'exotisme* to later, postcolonial variations on the term in the work of Glissant.

Poems from *Stèles* selected for the *Tout-Monde* anthology published in 2010 (a year before its editor's death) encapsulate the Segalenian exoticism with which Glissant engages across his work. In 'Conseils au bon voyageur', for instance, Segalen praises the permanent alternation implicit in the changing landscapes of travel, linking this to the 'the intoxicating eddies of the great river Diversity'; and in 'Nom caché', he challenges the Western privileging of knowledge, and gestures towards the power of identifying a place of opacity beyond comprehension, underlining a radical commitment to what Glissant would dub the 'right to opacity': 'may the devastating torrent come rather than Knowledge'.[28] Yvonne Hsieh notes that — in focusing on the key terms evident in these texts such as 'diversity' and 'opacity' — 'none has contributed as much as Glissant to the consecration of Segalen as a precursor of postcolonial thinking',[29] and it is true that the Martinican thinker appears to discern in works such as the *Essai sur l'exotisme* precursory concepts and embryonic debates foreshadowing phenomena that would emerge as central to postcolonialism and to considerations of postcoloniality, and might be seen as essential to a distinctively French and Francophone contribution to those fields.

As Marc Gontard comments, Segalen's association of intercultural contact with the 'imprévisible' (unpredictable) — a term particularly evident in *Equipée*, the hybrid travel narrative in which the aesthetics of diversity are sketched out and illustrated in the field — is key to understanding the distinction between Glissantian 'créolisation' and a more biological and predetermined process of 'métissage' (or at least between what Gontard sees as 'métissage acculturant' (acculturating hybridization) and 'métissage créolisant' (creolizing hybridization)).[30] Glissant notes: 'creolization is unpredictable whereas you could calculate the effects of hybridization' (*IPD*, 19), pointing towards the possibility in a period of globalization of the residually neguentropic cultural distinctiveness that Segalen himself sought in the texts produced in the final few years of his life when he identified discontinuity within apparent entropic continuity: 'new partitions and unforeseen lacunae, a system of very fine filigree striated through the fields that one initially perceived as an unbroken space' (*EE*, 57–8). In literary and linguistic terms, this observation is particularly evident in the recognition and celebration of multilingualism, that is in the 'mise en réseau' (networking) of languages to which Glissant alludes in *Introduction à une poétique du Divers*, and of which *Stèles* is a particularly striking example (*IPD*, 122). For Glissant, retention of diversity depends on recognition of what Silke Segler-Messner dubs 'multilingualism as the foundation of every form of writing', and it is in Segalen's work that he discovers a clear example of such a post–monolingual poetics that permits scrutiny from a postcolonial perspective of language use.[31]

Victor Segalen, Édouard Glissant and the Evolution of Postcolonial Theory

When Celia Britton's *Édouard Glissant and Postcolonial Theory* appeared in 1999, resistance in the French-speaking world to what is often perceived as the Anglo-Saxon import of postcolonial theory had been longstanding. This resistance should not, of course, be singularized, for it ranged from hostility towards approaches to literature viewed as anti-universalist, moving via a sense that postcolonialism had merely recreated critical practices long evident in France (in works such as Bernard Mouralis's *Les Contre-littératures* (1975)), to a wholly justified frustration that critical models generated outside the Francosphere were inadequate to understandings of the French-speaking world.[32] Jean-Marc Moura's *Littératures francophones et théorie postcoloniale* (published by PUF in the same year as *Édouard Glissant and Postcolonial Theory*) represented a notable exception in its effort to analyse the potential contribution of postcolonial theory to readings of Francophone literature.[33] However, whereas Moura's work tends to cast postcolonial literature in French as a passive recipient of work originating in the Anglophone academy, Celia Britton's sustained and rigorous study of Glissant stressed the potentially active contribution of Francophone writing from the Caribbean to postcolonial theory itself. As such, it represented a most timely intervention, not least because it formed part of a diverse cluster of texts — including other studies, such as Peter Hallward's *Absolutely Postcolonial* (2001)[34] — that challenged the monolingual *impasse* into which postcolonialism risked retreating around the turn of the century: on the one hand, Britton revealed the substantial insights offered by the body of Glissantian work, theoretical and fictional, as the field of French studies was slowly 'postcolonialized'; on the other, she underlined the then restricted nature of postcolonial criticism and the need to open this up to a wider range of references from different cultural and linguistic traditions beyond those regularly recycled.

Britton began her study by identifying in Glissant's work a terminological coherence; previous English-language critics and translators had tended to rely on a less stable range of terms. She argued that if Glissant were to be validated and recognized as a postcolonial theorist in his own right and his thought integrated into more widespread reflections on postcoloniality, then concepts central to his work, those of 'Relation', 'essence', 'opacity', and 'detour', should be granted wider resonance. As the title suggested, *Édouard Glissant and Postcolonial Theory* situated its subject for the first time in relation to postcolonialism, and explored the overlap of its subject's work with that of Fanon, Said, Bhabha, Spivak and the other then prominent theorists of postcolonialism, stressing the ways in which the Martinican intellectual inhabited a similar if not entirely identical intellectual world as them. However, in Britton's study, Glissant's specificity is constantly stressed, and there is no easy conflation of radically different cultural or political situations, no attempt, for instance, to overlay Spivak's Indian subcontinent on Glissant's Martinique. As a result, it is the divergences rather than the similarities on which *Édouard Glissant and Postcolonial Theory* focuses, on the slippage between, for example, Fanon's and Glissant's approaches to delirium and madness. The study unfolds subtly, interweaving theoretical considerations with fresh and original readings of Glissant's novels. As is suggested above, Glissant's work privileges in particular the role of language as a key element of postcolonial experience. Fictional texts, as working models of counterpoetics, are seen to illustrate strategies of resistance.[35]

Britton underlined the conceptual coherence of Glissant's work, by 1999 an *œuvre* already spanning a period of almost fifty years. His novels and essays in particular are seen to constitute a unified struggle to forge new modes of expression whose implications ultimately transcend the particular situation of Martinique and also of the French Caribbean more generally. The final chapter, drawing on Glissant's work from the 1990s, accordingly outlined a new world-view, rooted in the Caribbean but based on an understanding of the distinctively Segalenian concepts of diversity and unpredictability whose wider implications for a postcolonial grasp of language and identity were then only slowly emerging. In the opening chapter of *Édouard Glissant and Postcolonial Theory*, 'Concepts of Resistance', Britton acknowledges the formative role of Segalen in her subject's thought. The Breton author (as discussed by Glissant in *L'Intention poétique*) is read in the light of Spivak's work. His 'wish [evident in some of the early, Polynesian texts] to lose himself in a completely alien culture' is seen, however, as a form of bad faith — that is, in Britton's terms, 'the fantasy of absolute otherness absolves him of the responsibility of examining his position in relation to it — of becoming aware of his own positionality as investigative subject' (*EGPT*, 17). 'Relation' and 'opacité' are seen as alternative mechanisms adopted by Glissant to safeguard the other's difference and avoid the assimilative extremes of exoticism. (Such extremes are reflected in the spectrum described in *Lire l'exotisme* by Jean-Marc Moura, a spectrum that ranges, at one extreme, from absorption or assimilation of otherness to, at the other, the loss of self.[36]) In Britton's formulation: 'just as I cannot reduce the Other to my norms, nor conversely can I *become* the Other, in the kind of exoticizing identification that Glissant attributes to Segalen (of whom he writes [in *Poétique de la Relation*] that "personally I believe he died of the Other's opacity")' (*EGPT*, 19).

Although the references to Segalen in *Édouard Glissant and Postcolonial Theory* are restricted to these two occasions, what emerges from these is a very clear sense — in the frame of postcolonial theory — of the ambiguous nature of Glissant's dialogue with this interlocutor. The rapport between Glissant and Segalen is seen as deeply formative in the ways outlined above, yet is at the same time characterized by a dialectical process of self-differentiation as the Martinican thinker progressively distanced himself from the work of the earlier twentieth-century naval doctor and precocious theorist of the exotic. (Jean-Louis Joubert eloquently describes Glissant's relationship to Segalen as that of a 'critical reader of [his] works and sometimes [his] heir, natural or paradoxical'.[37]) It is undeniable, for instance, that 'relation' and 'opacité', despite their clear distinctiveness and their specific point of genesis in a Caribbean context, owe much to Segalenian concepts such as 'le Divers' (Diversity), 'l'impénétrabilité' (impenetrability) and 'incompréhensibilité éternelle' (eternal incomprehensibility), as set out in the essay on exoticism. Such a debt is made particularly clear, from the title itself even, in the 1996 volume *Introduction à une poétique du Divers*, where Glissant writes: 'Honour and respect to Segalen. He was the first to raise the issue of diversity in the world, to fight exoticism as a complacent form of colonization, and he was a doctor on a military vessel' (*IPD*, 76–7). Segalen's early twentieth-century analysis of the decline of cultural difference — 'Diversity is in decline. Therein lies the great earthly threat. It is therefore against this decay that we must fight, fight amongst ourselves — perhaps die with beauty' (*EE*, 63) — resonates with Glissant's critique of assimilation in the post-departmentalized Caribbean. Segalen had also firmly, and somewhat surprisingly, been associated by Glissant in the 1950s with struggles for decolonization: 'There are innumerable people suffering and dying today for their Difference to be acknowledged, so that Diversity can emerge again *in reality*. Perhaps he would have allied himself to them, or supported their struggle' (*IP*, 101–2).

There is, however, a clear shift. Glissant's later readings become more nuanced, and Segalen is presented in *Le Discours antillais* as 'le partagé' (the divided one), an enlightened thinker who to an extent transcends the constraints of his early twentieth-century context, engages differently with otherness, but cannot entirely escape the dilemmas of his contemporary socio-political circumstances. In the terms already evident in *L'Intention poétique*, Glissant notes: 'il n'était pas de Pékin mais de Brest, et non pas Chinois du Vieil Empire mais Français du début de ce siècle'[38] (he was not from Beijing but from Brest, and not Chinese of the Old Empire but French from the beginning of this century). Nevertheless, this is not a rejection of Segalen, but rather an assertion of his ambiguously precursory status, '*en avant* du monde' (*ahead* of the world) — that is, as one of the 'premiers poètes de la Relation' (first poets of Relating), emblematic of the modernist trajectory from centre to periphery, yet excluded from the radical decentred-ness of 'Relation', distanced from the creolization that the ultimate essentialism of Segalenian diversity belies, from the systems of plurality and hybridity that Segalen could perhaps not imagine. In a discussion of Segalen and Saint-John Perse, Glissant points even in the life and work of the former to a dislocation between poetic aspirations and a lived context in which such aspirations remains largely unthinkable: 'I myself believe that he died of the opacity of the Other, of the impossibility he had discovered of perfecting the transmutation of which he dreamed.'[39]

In refusing to simplify Segalen, and in accordingly facing the inherent contradictions of his work, Glissant proposes an investigation of the aesthetics of diversity that is simultaneously historical and actual. He examines the colonial context in which it is mired (a dimension distinctly missing from the postmodern interpretations of a reader such as Baudrillard), but also understands the postcolonial context in which it has come to prominence. Glissant's engagement with Segalen is, therefore, not so much an extension or a completion of works such as the *Essai sur l'exotisme* — a text which, as Cornille notes, '[i]n its fundamental incompleteness (...) only asked to be continued' (MC, 172) — as their recasting, translation and re-interpretation in a contemporary frame.

Conclusion: From Anxieties of Influence to Progenerative Thought

Celia Britton describes the task of the postcolonial critic as levering open the ideological closures of dominant discourses, locating moments of fracture, and 'uncover[ing] the subject-position assigned to the subaltern in the text [and showing] how this may involve deconstructing a Western logic of representation and self-representation' (*EGPT*, 57). This is a concise definition of one of the principal aims of postcolonial theory itself, and one to which Glissant, in his literary, philosophical and political writings, contributed greatly. The conclusion to *Édouard Glissant and Postcolonial Theory* signals Glissant's critical and theoretical engagement with what Britton calls 'the monolithic hegemony of "sameness"', describing the ways in which contemporary recognition of chaos, creolization, the rhizome, *archipélisation* and the *Tout-Monde* betoken the end of 'old, singular system[s] of domination' and the emergence of 'a world view based on diversity and unpredictability' (*EGPT*, 179). In understanding the genealogy of Glissant's thought — and, it might be suggested, of postcolonial thought more generally — identifying the constructive yet ultimately ambivalent role of Segalen continues to be key. The sense of a community of thinkers that such dialoguing may be seen to assemble is not, however, to be understood either in terms of descent and influence, or of genealogies and sequentially linear connexions. To borrow from a distinction proposed by the anthropologist Tim Ingold, it is perhaps more helpfully interpreted (and here in actively Glissantian terms) as 'relational' more than in terms of 'relatedness', for such a 'relational' approach challenges notions of chronological precedence and reveals the ways in which the work of a thinker and creator such as Segalen can be grasped more dynamically, beyond the immediate temporal and ideological niche from which it emerged.[40]

Ingold explores questions of cultural and biological ancestry, drawing not on Glissant but on Deleuze and Guattari (whose role in Glissant's thought is well recorded) in order to replace conventional genealogical models with a rhizomatic alternative, 'a dense and tangled cluster of interlaced threads or filaments, any point in which can be pointed to any other' (*PE*, 140). This anti-genealogy leads to a 'progenerative' model that — if applied to intellectual communities — challenges quasi-biological ideas of descent as well as the anxieties of influence that these may betoken (and that are often evident in accounts of Francophone Caribbean thought). Instead, it permits the acknowledgement of different, relational understandings within the evolution of an interrelated body of thinking, 'the continual unfolding of an entire field of relationships' (*PE*, 142). As such, challenging the reductive causality of reception and influence permits a more fluid understanding of cross-generational, even transhistorical dialogues. It underlines — in the case of Segalen and Glissant — not only the role of the work of the former in the elaboration of the conceptual apparatus of the latter, but also the heuristic value of such re-engagement in recontextualizing and illuminating meanings previously obscured.

In the light of such a reading, Cornille's identification of Segalen as the 'theoretical zombie of Glissantian discourse', and his associated re-statement on the part of Glissant of an anxiety of influence (MC, 174, 173), seem overegged and ultimately unfounded. Cornille's insistent identification of Segalen as a 'présence incontournable' (unavoidable presence) in Glissant's work — 'eventually exasperating, we sense, as there is no way to express anything that has not been proposed by his predecessor' — fails to acknowledge that more complex processes are at play. Marc Gontard provides a much clearer sense of what is at stake in Segalen's absorption in contemporary Francophone Caribbean thought. Including in his discussion of this network the *Créolistes*, who have been similarly attentive to Segalen's work (Chamoiseau includes the *Essai sur l'exotisme* in his *sentimentèque*, and most probably encountered this work via Glissant), Gontard notes:

If Caribbean people have found in the work of this Breton a writer of otherness who has enriched their thought, the system of creolization they have imagined provides a response to Segalenian fear about entropy by making archipelago-ness an elastic figure of discontinuous being.[41]

To present the intellectual work encapsulated in the encounter of Glissant and Segalen in such progenerative terms is also to provide a further (and, in the case of a Caribbean thinker such as Glissant, highly suggestive) gloss to Edward Said's reflections on the secular critics. A figure such as Glissant is located as a result firmly and constructively between processes of 'filiation' (in which intellectuals are linked closely to a place of origin 'by birth, nationality, profession') and of 'affiliation' (in which critics seeks new alliances and allegiances 'by social and political conviction, economic and historical circumstances, voluntary effort and willed deliberation').[42]

These relationships, bridging the gap between 'filiation' (connexions within the Caribbean and the wider Americas) and 'affiliation' (encapsulated by mature Glissantian concepts such as the 'Tout-Monde') are illustrated and exemplified by Glissant's dynamic and evolving engagement with Segalen. This encounter may at the same time be seen as generative of alternative modes of thinking such as *Antillanité* (Caribbeanness), and as key to understanding the Martinican thinker's complex negotiation of his own location between

the historical *Négritude* of Aimé Césaire and the *Créolité* of the generation that followed him. Therefore, the significant rendezvous between
Segalen and Glissant is not — to return to James Clifford's terms, to
which I alluded at the opening of this article — so much *manqué*, as
indirect and prolonged; it provides a compelling illustration of Khatibi's model of critical distancing and interpretative absorption, and also
of Borges's understanding of reading as a process of progressive and
repeated engagement accompanied by evolving comprehension.[43]

NOTES

1   Victor Segalen, *Essay on Exoticism: An Aesthetics of Diversity*, translated by Yaël
    Rachel Schlick (Durham, NC and London: Duke University Press, 2002),
    63. Henceforward referred to as *EE*.
2   Édouard Glissant, *Introduction à une poétique du Divers* (Paris: Gallimard, 1996),
    98. Henceforward referred to as *IPD*. Unless otherwise stated, all translations
    are my own.
3   Cited by Andrew Harvey and Ian Watson, 'Introduction' in Victor Segalen,
    Paintings, translated by Andrew Harvey and Ian Watson (London: Quartet
    Books, 1991), vii–ix (vi).
4   James Clifford, *The Predicament of Culture: Twentieth-Century Ethnography,
    Literature, and Art* (Cambridge, MA: Harvard University Press, 1988), 152.
5   On this term, see Charles Forsdick and David Murphy, 'The Rise of
    the Francophone Postcolonial Intellectual: The Emergence of a Tradition',
    Modern and Contemporary France 17:2 (2009), 163–75.
6   Sidi Omar Azeroual, 'Le contraire et le semblable' in *Le Clézio, Glissant,
    Segalen: la quête comme déconstruction de l'aventure* (Chambéry: Éditions de
    l'université de Savoie, 2011), 97–106 (99). This volume will henceforward
    be referred to as *LGS*.
7   Azeroual, 'Le contraire et le semblable', 103.
8   Jean-Louis Cornille, 'La mémoire courte des poètes immémoriaux (Glissant
    et Segalen)' in *Plagiat et créativité: (treize enquêtes sur l'auteur et son autre)*
    (Amsterdam: Rodopi, 2008), 171–82. Henceforward referred to as MC.
9   Cited by Michel Le Bris, 'Présentation' in Victor Segalen, *Voyages au pays du
    réel: œuvres littéraires* (Brussels: Complexe, 1995), 7–27 (11).
10 http://www.potomitan.info/chamoiseau/glissant.php/, consulted 7 February
    2014. Chamoiseau also includes Faulkner, Fanon and Wilfredo Lam as key
    influences.
11 Celia Britton, *Edouard Glissant and Postcolonial Theory* (Charlottesville:
    University of Virginia Press, 1999), 13. Henceforward referred to as *EGPT*.
12 Victor Segalen, *L'Intention poétique* (Paris: Seuil, 1969), 95–103.
    Henceforward referred to as *IP*.

13   Cornille notes an accumulation of formal resonances between *Stèles* and *Les Indes*, and comments that Segalen's work appears to function for Glissant as 'a model of poetic ordering, an example of composition of a collection, generating a seductive publishing fantasy' (MC, 177). Yvonne Hsieh similarly discusses these points of convergence in 'A poetics of relationality: Victor Segalen's *Stèles*' in *Empire Lost: France and its Other Worlds*, edited by Elisabeth Mudimbe-Boyi (Lanham, MD and Plymouth, UK: Lexington Books, 2009), 89–104 (90).

14   Édouard Glissant, *Les Entretiens de Baton Rouge, avec Alexandre Leupin* (Paris: Gallimard, 2008), and *Entretiens avec Lise Gauvin (1991–2009)* (Paris: Gallimard, 2010). The latter will henceforward be referred to as *ELG*.

15   Édouard Glissant and Patrick Chamoiseau, *Quand les murs tombent* (Paris: Galaade, 2008).

16   Édouard Glissant, *La Terre, le feu, l'eau et les vents* (Paris: Galaade, 2010), 93–6. On the intellectual work of Glissant's final decade, see Charles Forsdick, 'Late Glissant: History, "World Literature", and the Persistence of the Political', *Small Axe* 14:3 (2010), 121–34.

17   Norge, 'Le souffle coupé', *Europe* 696 (1987), 146–7 (146).

18   Victor Segalen, *Œuvres complètes*, edited by Henry Bouillier, 2 volumes (Paris: Laffont, 1995). A project to publish a new, multi-volume *Complete Works* with Champion has been underway for several years, directed by the comparatist and Segalenian Philippe Postel.

19   Timothy Billings and Christopher Bush, 'Introduction' in Victor Segalen, *Stèles*, translated and annotated by Timothy Billings and Christopher Bush (Middletown, CT: Wesleyan University Press, 2007), 1–45 (3).

20   Silke Segler-Messner, 'Victor Segalen et la poétique de l'altérité dans la théorie littéraire postcoloniale (Glissant, Khatibi)' in *Voyages à l'envers. Formes et figures de l'exotisme dans les littératures post-coloniales francophones*, edited by Silke Segler-Messner (Strasbourg: Presses universitaires de Strasbourg, 2009), 69–86 (84).

21   On this subject, see Charles Forsdick, '"L'exote mangé par les hommes"' in *Reading Diversity*, edited by Charles Forsdick and Susan Marson (Glasgow: University of Glasgow French and German Publications, 2000), 5–24.

22   Jean Scemla, 'Entretien avec Khatibi', *Bulletin de l'Association Victor Segalen* 2 (1989), 9–10 (9).

23   Abdelkebir Khatibi, *La Mémoire tatouée* (Paris: Denoël, 1971), 124.

24   It is perhaps surprising that Glissant, as a Caribbean intellectual, engages more with the later Segalen — associated with the 'Chinese cycle' of his work — than with the earlier texts such as *Les Immémoriaux* relating to Polynesia and the island cultures and archipelagos of the Pacific Ocean. Although the 1955 edition presented three works inspired by China, Pierre Jean Jouve's preface makes telling references to the Polynesian *roman ethnographique* (ethnographic

novel), and parallels between the Caribbean and the Pacific inform Glissant's work such as *Poétique de la Relation*, in which he notes: 'The archipelagic reality, in the Caribbean or in the Pacific, illustrates naturally the thinking of Relation' (Édouard Glissant, *Poétique de la Relation* (Paris: Gallimard, 1990), 46). It is striking that one of Glissant's final texts — the vicarious travel narrative *La Terre magnétique: les errances de Rapa-Nui, l'île de Pâques* (Paris: Seuil, 2007) — permitted full engagement with Polynesia fifty years after the first encounter with Segalen.

25 Jean-Pol Madou, 'Le germe et le rhizome' in *LGS*, 73–80 (75).

26 The *équipée* is a form of digressive mobility described by Segalen in his travel narrative of the same title; although associated in particular with Patrick Chamoiseau, the *driveur* (embodiment of the *drive* and a concrete manifestation of *errance*) is a key figure in two of Glissant's novels, *Malemort* and *La Case du commandeur*: through constant movement, the *drive* permits resistance, challenging not least the forms of immobility imposed by plantation societies.

27 Édouard Glissant, *Soleil de la conscience* (Paris: Seuil, 1956), 11.

28 Glissant, *La Terre, le feu, l'eau et les vents*, 96. Translations taken from Segalen, *Stèles*, translated and annotated by Billings and Bush, 199, 257.

29 Hsieh, 'A poetics of relationality', 90.

30 Marc Gontard, 'Victor Segalen: de l'altérité à l'archipélité' in *L'Imaginaire de l'archipel*, edited by Georges Voisset (Paris: Karthala, 2003), 165–76 (175).

31 Silke Segler-Messner, 'Victor Segalen et la poétique de l'altérité', 84. On post-monolingualism, see Yasemin Yildiz, *Beyond the Mother Tongue: The Post-Monolingual Condition* (New York: Fordham University Press, 2012).

32 Bernard Mouralis, *Les Contre-littératures* (Paris: Presses universitaires de France, 1975).

33 Jean-Marc Moura, *Littératures francophones et théorie postcoloniale* (Paris: Presses universitaires de France, 1999).

34 Peter Hallward, *Absolutely Postcolonial: Writing Between the Singular and the Specific* (Manchester: Manchester University Press, 2001).

35 These are strategies evident also, I would suggest, in Segalenian works such as *Les Immémoriaux* and *Stèles*, that is, of establishing 'a relationship of resistance and subversion *to* the dominant language (. . .) negotiated from the inside'. It is such strategies that may also be seen to link the poetics of opacity evident in certain works by Segalen and Glissant, with texts such as *Les Immémoriaux* and *Malemort* actively disorientating the reader, confronting him with what Virginie Turcotte describes as 'a cultural otherness by deporting him to an elsewhere he does not know' (Virginie Turcotte, 'Figures de l'altérité: du regard occidental sur la Polynésie aux réflexions de Segalen et Glissant' in *Désert, nomadisme, altérité*, edited by Rachel Bouvet, Jean-François Gaudreau and Virginie Turcotte (Montreal: Figura, 2000), 149–85 (150)).

36 Jean-Marc Moura, *Lire l'exotisme* (Paris: Dunod, 1992).

37 Jean-Louis Joubert, 'Poétique de l'exotisme: Saint-John Perse, Victor Segalen et Édouard Glissant', *Cahiers du CRLH* 5 (1988), 281–95.

38 Glissant, *Poétique de la Relation*, 195.

39 Glissant, *Poétique de la Relation*, 207.

40 Tim Ingold, 'Ancestry, generation, substance, memory, land' in *The Perception of the Environment: Essays in Livelihood, Dwelling and Skill* (London: Routledge, 2000), 132–51. Henceforward referred to as *PE*.

41 Marc Gontard, 'Victor Segalen: de l'altérité a l'archipélité', 165–76 (176).

42 Edward W. Said, *The World, the Text and the Critic* (Cambridge, MA: Harvard University Press, 1983), 24–5.

43 This article was completed while I was Arts and Humanities Research Council Theme Leadership Fellow for 'Translating Cultures' (AH/K503381/1), and I record my thanks to the AHRC for its support.

'Internal Harmony, Peace to the Outside World': Imagining Community in Nineteenth-Century Haiti

Kate Hodgson

Abstract:

This article explores the idea of community and 'internal concord' in a radically divided, post-independence Haiti. As the country negotiated the process of decolonization from France, Haitian political writings and speeches repeatedly returned to the problem of how a truly united Haiti might be envisaged. These reworkings of the idea of community were instrumental in the work of postcolonial nation-building in Haiti in the first half of the nineteenth century. Yet the publication of Haiti's *Rural Code* in 1826 gives a different perspective on the process of national construction of community through work, particularly agricultural labour. The article seeks to look beyond the ideals of unity and Concordia which were being vigorously proclaimed at the time, in order to understand the impact of questions of work and worklessness on political discourse surrounding the idea of postcolonial community in nineteenth-century Haiti.

Keywords: Haiti, community, postcolonial, work, worklessness, nation, Concordia, Rural Code, pre-colonial

The French abolitionist Victor Schœlcher's trenchant criticism of nineteenth-century Haiti as 'an agglomeration of men rather than a society' summarizes the problem of understanding the functioning of the newly independent state.[1] From Schœlcher's perspective, Haiti seemed a chaotic 'agglomeration', a confused mass with no ordering principles. This viewpoint is, unsurprisingly, influenced by

Paragraph 37.2 (2014): 178–192
DOI: 10.3366/para.2014.0120
© Edinburgh University Press
www.euppublishing.com/para

colonial ideas of what constituted an ordered and 'civilized' society. Schœlcher saw France's colonies as forming part of the national community, regulated by a 'common pact' with metropolitan France, and his aim in seeking to abolish slavery was to bring all inhabitants of the colonies into this pact.[2] Haiti did not align with Schœlcher's model of a functioning community, not solely due to the domestic political divisions that he noticed during his visit, but also because it did not fit within his broader organizing framework of ideas: it was 'dis-ordered' both internally and internationally. Schœlcher's harshest criticism was reserved for the country's leadership: 'Shame on those in power, not on the people' (II, 207). Subsequent external perspectives on Haiti have echoed his judgement, and his frustration.

The problem of defining what exactly a community is — the space it occupies, which groups within a diverse and often divided national context are given a stake in its functioning, and how it is controlled — goes to the heart of this article. It seeks to reconcile the call for internal harmony of the title, taken from President Boyer's 1825 'Proclamation to the people and the army', with the successive difficulties faced by post-revolutionary Haiti in creating an ideal of community that would bring together opposing factions within the national territory.

The question of unity had been instrumental throughout the revolution, as internal conflict threatened to break apart the 'indigenous army' (*armée indigène*) in their battles against the French.[3] In July 1803, according to Haitian historian Thomas Madiou, Jean-Jacques Dessalines delivered a speech in Creole to his soldiers, in which he called for the past to be forgotten and for black and mixed-race Haitians to come together under his command: 'My brothers, let us forget the past; let us forget those awful days, when led astray by the whites, we took up arms against one another'.[4] In its appeal for internal unity, this speech designated a number of clear external enemies — most obviously the Europeans and remaining white Creoles of the colony, but also two rival armed factions of 'Congos', led by Lamour Dérance and Petit Noël Prière, who could through their insurgency 'compromise the cause of liberty'.[5] According to Madiou, Dérance and his African-born followers had no interest in uniting with the revolutionary leaders to found a new nation; instead they wanted to continue their independent existence. The motto inscribed upon the Haitian flag, 'Strength in Unity', reinforced the attempt at a unifying message, as did the 1804 declaration of independence in which Dessalines, Pétion, Christophe and the other revolutionary generals pronounced 'the oath which is to unite us'.[6]

In spite of these repeated calls for unity, the new state splintered soon after independence. Dessalines was assassinated in 1806, and during the crucial nation-building period of 1806–20 Haiti effectively became two countries: a republic under Pétion in the South and a monarchy under Christophe in the North. When Christophe's reign ended in 1820, the new president, Jean-Pierre Boyer based his vision for the future of the country in propaganda and speeches calling, once again, for unity. To this end he toured the country, holding banquets for the country's principal generals and magistrates in an attempt to unify the fractured whole. These were extensively reported in the national press: in May 1821 the Haitian newspaper *La Concorde* reproduced a list of patriotic toasts made on one such occasion, including the following by General Prévost: 'To Union, to Harmony, to Concordia, to Friendship, to Fraternity, may they unite all Haitians forever!'[7] In 1825, on the occasion of the recognition of Haitian independence by France, Boyer called again for internal harmony or Concordia.[8] This proclamation was both an exercise in political rhetoric and an attempt to convince the entire population of the island to work (to work together, but above all to work) to achieve the kind of economic growth necessary to pay off the debt of 150 million francs that he had just contracted to the former colonial power.[9]

Yet can any kind of national community be said to have existed in Haiti in the early nineteenth century, outside of the state-led rhetoric of Concordia? What was at stake in the idea of the nation was significantly different among different groups: not just because of the national split between 1807 and 1820 and its repercussions, but also due to the profound class and colour divides noted by historians of Haiti.[10] Fick depicts the nation as fundamentally splintered and divided at the end of the revolution, with groups of armed 'Congos' like Dérance and his followers choosing to maintain their liberty in the hills and remote borderlands of Haiti.[11] Any attempt by the elite to counter the radical refusal of these groups to lose their hard-fought freedom, in order to effect their integration into the Haitian peasantry and promote it in terms of creating one whole national community, inevitably compromised expressions of 'unity'. While the existence of outlaw or rebel groups does not invalidate the concept of a political or national community in itself, the visible presence of a radical rejection of state authority in nineteenth-century Haiti was compounded by the existence of complex, widespread and profound divisions existing on multiple levels between state and people, urban and rural groups, mulatto and black, literate and illiterate, Creoles and

Africans (also called 'Bossales' or 'Congos'), former slaves and former *affranchis*, etc.

This article examines how the idea of community (or plural communities) was imagined and written about in independent Haiti by the first generation of Haitians after the revolution. It aims to foreground the idea that these imaginings were not always reflective of wider popular understandings of community, nor reflected in different groups within Haitian society at large. As such it is inevitably more of a history of the *ideas* of community in early post-colonial Haiti dreamt up by the governors, that partially or entirely obscure the realities of the governed. The rhetoric of community, within the plantation or agricultural environment and on a national scale, was central to the work of nation-building in Haiti, and the development of the 1826 *Rural Code* underpins my understanding of the organization of the post-colonial Haitian state. Another focal point of my analysis is the importance of the past and of myth in creating an ideal of community in Haiti, to which the present was unfavourably compared.

Prompted by the work of Celia Britton on community in a Francophone Caribbean context, and by the work of historians of Haiti such as Gérard Barthélémy on the *moun andeyo*, the rural, peasant communities of 'people outside' or excluded from the Haitian national body politic, this article reconsiders post-colonial communities from the point of view of the first state in the Francophone world to negotiate the process of (early, contested and problematic) decolonization.

Theories of Community

Community can be determined firstly in terms of people and their investment in the intimate spaces they inhabit, and secondly in terms of interrelationships on a larger scale between different groups with different goals and interests. Both the national space and internal relationships are vital in understanding the idea of community in early post-colonial Haiti. Celia Britton has examined the idea of community in terms of the theoretical representation of Caribbean plantation societies. Based on a consideration of race, assimilation and (post-)colonial relationships between Europe and the Caribbean, she suggests that in this context 'community cannot be taken for granted; it must be consciously constructed as a political act'.[12] How was Haiti constructed as a community from within by its early politicians and writers? Whose idea of community? If this cannot be considered an accurate representation of everyone 'within', how can 'the problem of community' be resolved? Britton's *The Sense of Community* also usefully takes up Jean-Luc Nancy's *The Inoperative Community* (*La Communauté désœuvrée*) in a Caribbean, post-slavery and post-colonial context, with particular regard to community myths and their connexion to work. These ideas take on new significance in the context of nineteenth-century Haiti, where the notion of work as a form of community participation was particularly problematic, constituting one of the most radical sources of division and conflict within both local and national communities. The relationship between work and community, with particular reference to the idea of 'inoperative' or 'unworked' community, as Britton's alternative translation of Nancy's title has it, is examined in the context of Haiti's *Rural Code*. Contrasting perceptions of work in this period clearly show up the cracks in the national narrative, with a parallel perspective on small-scale, community initiatives in recent historical studies. Finally, another significant nineteenth-century perspective on work and 'worklessness' is considered: the myth of origins in the work of a number of nineteenth-century Haitian writers and intellectuals, centred on the island's Amerindian past.

The idea of the nation as a focal point of community concentrated in one political territory has been described by Minar and Greer as 'a feeling of identity, shared fate, common loyalty'.[13] Benedict Anderson has also famously considered the nation to be an 'imagined community', located within 'cultural artefacts' such as newspapers which in both expressing and embodying a collective sense of nationhood carry their own charge of 'emotional legitimacy'.[14] Nancy also considers the impact of print culture in his theories of community, stating in an article appearing in English in 1992 that the 'in-common' is both buried and 'totally, invincibly, present' in the written word, and referring to 'a community of concepts, of culture, of history'.[15] The national community and the written word are thus inseparably linked at their origin.

The importance of print culture in the early creation and publicizing of the 'concept' of the Haitian nation state has been examined by Jenson, who shows how Haiti promoted itself beyond its borders by sending out printed copies of its Proclamation of Independence worldwide. She stresses the legitimacy of these national cultural artefacts as a post-revolutionary response to the slave culture of the Americas at the time.[16] The language in the prologue to the Haitian Declaration of Independence and in speeches by Dessalines demonstrates the importance of a shared identity based on freedoms won and common loyalty in the face of oppression. This is expressed in stirring nationalist addresses to the citizens of the newly-created country and in printed documents, used by the elite of both North and South to attempt to create national community in the eyes of the world. In the face of French accusations that Haitian writings were a fabrication by British abolitionists, it was a point of pride for Haiti to have its own national press, as Vastey noted: 'We write and we publish. Even in its infancy, our nation has produced poets and writers'.[17]

As well as contributing to the external promotion of Haiti's national image, the national press also took on the role of internal unifying force. The stated mission of King Christophe's newspaper in the North, the *Gazette Royale d'Hayti*, for example, was to contribute to 'the complete extinction of civil war and the reunion of Haitians of all colours as part of one single family, under the monarchical and paternal government of his Majesty Henry I'.[18] Yet it should be stressed that despite the rhetoric of the nation-as-family, the print culture of early nineteenth-century Haiti was produced and consumed solely by a tiny literate minority within the country. The masses were again excluded (*andeyo*) from active participation in this form of production of national community.

It is difficult, but also useful to look beyond national unities which are being so vigorously proclaimed through print culture, in order to understand how the idea of community functioned in reality in both domestic and foreign politics. Nancy has examined how the idea of community necessarily excludes as well as includes within its boundaries: 'Such exclusion can be named distinction, exile, banishment, sacrifice, disdain (...). At the bottom, that which the community wants to exclude is that which does not let itself be identified in it. We call it the "other".'[19] The exclusion or 'othering' of both external and internal elements that had explicitly rejected 'common being' with the new nation (France and other foreign powers; certain African-born internal groups such as those led by Lamour Dérance and Petit Noël Prière) allowed Haiti to begin to construct its rhetoric of national unity and community. The rhetorical creation of national community through print culture, through evocation of a shared national revolutionary past, through exclusion of identified 'others' and through the message of unity through work contributed to shaping the message of 'internal harmony' or

Concordia, as it was termed in Boyer's 1825 speech. This constitutive feature of the Haitian nationalist ideal provides a vantage-point from which to examine a range of competing understandings of community in Haiti in the nineteenth century.

Concordia: Independent Haiti, the Rural Code and Internal Harmony

The idea of the nation was heavily promoted by the educated elite in nineteenth-century Haiti in order to create a narrative of internal harmony. Boyer's plea for national harmony fits into this framework as a plea for a shared and consensual version of the historic heritage to be passed down to future generations. 'Our glorious nationality in the middle of the ruins of the colonial aristocracy', begins Madiou's *History of Haiti*.[20] Boyer's 1825 speech to the people of Haiti offers an insight into national identity and values from the perspective of the elite: he cites commerce and agriculture as shared concerns, an attachment to national institutions, shared rights (threatened from outside the community, rather than from within), and above all national unity. He calls on the nation to continue to uphold these principles in order to sustain an enduring legacy for Haiti's future. The evocation of external threats to Haitian freedoms aims to strengthen national solidarity, and Boyer claims that it is 'through union' or Concordia (etymologically, hearts together — *con-cor*) that Haitians will best be able to protect themselves from outsiders who would challenge their rights.

Yet one of the major challenges facing Haiti in its post-colonial existence was at its very heart — namely, the underlying social and colour divisions between different factions inherited from the colonial era and from the Haitian revolution. The ground had already been laid for the ongoing resistance of the black masses against plantation labour during the revolutionary period. Despite the attempts of French commissioner Polverel and Governor Toussaint Louverture to maintain the prosperity of Saint Domingue's sugar plantations after the abolition of slavery in 1793, plantation labour was consistently experienced as a continuation of slavery by the African-born majority. After independence, these non-property-owning Africans and their descendents would constitute the earliest generation of the *moun andeyo*, the excluded masses that the new Haitian state attempted to tie to the land by both legal and military means. Along with the construction of military fortifications, the maintenance of national agriculture was a priority for the Haitian state from its earliest days, and manpower was needed for both. However, alternative communities emerged in the form of rural *Lakou* which challenged the fragile national hegemony by creating 'a very different social order', based on a self-regulated extended family structure.[21] According to Barthélemy, the first half-century of Haitian history can be summarized as the failed attempts of the State to maintain the black rural masses as agricultural labourers on nationalized plantations, and the contrasting success of the *Lakou* in creating multiple alternative communities via a 'counter-strategy of smallholdings'.[22]

In this early nineteenth-century world the prominence of borders, internal and external, exposes the Haitian elite's preoccupation with belonging, inclusion and the limits of the nation state. The external border with the Spanish slave colony of Santo Domingo was particularly contested during this period. In a text published in 1817, Christophe's publicist the Baron de Vastey described a group of Haitian and Dominican workers meeting at the border, working alongside one another, buying and selling goods in the marketplace, and then separating at the end of the day, the Haitians marching off to their side of the border, singing songs and beating drums, the Dominicans 'dancing gravely to the sound of their guitars' as they returned to slavery on the other side.[23] Preoccupied with the creation of a distinctive Haitian national community, Vastey downplays the cross-border relationships created through shared labour, instead emphasizing the integrity of national boundaries in order to protect Haitian sovereignty and reassure European powers that Haiti was not a threat to their slave colonies.[24] Yet Haiti's annexation of the Eastern side of the island soon after in 1822 leads us to reconsider these fragile concepts of 'external' and 'internal'. Although for Vastey the guitars of Dominican slavery and the drums of Haitian freedom failed to 'harmonize' across the border, the role of labour was key in defining their relationship and would remain so from the perspective of the State, once the whole island was under Haitian governance.

Overriding state concern regarding Haiti's declining agricultural production should be understood as a major driving force behind calls for national solidarity such as President Boyer's 1825 speech, prefaced by the promise that 'Commerce and agriculture will be expanded'.[25] The following year, the *Rural Code* was made law. The new legislation, applicable throughout the entire, now-unified island, called upon all citizens to support the state 'either through their services or through their industry'.[26] The flow of labour was controlled through internal borders between urban and rural spaces. According to the terms of the 1826 *Rural Code*, agricultural labourers were maintained on the land and were not allowed to resettle in urban areas unless they were accorded a special authorization by the magistrate of the rural district they wished to leave.[27] Those who could not prove other employment were obliged to cultivate the land, as agriculture was a protected domain of interest of the State. All those not conforming to the legislation of the Code were considered to be 'vagabonds' under the terms of the law, and an 'encouragement prize' was set up, to be awarded to the grower of the best nationalized produce in Haiti. The intention was to nationalize and standardize agricultural production, applicable to all landowners and peasants, as well as to make it more difficult for workers to leave the land.

The *Rural Code* was a continuation in many ways of the attempts of the ruling elite to link unity, work and freedom conceptually as key attributes of Haitian national community, now incorporating the entire island. Noting that the Eastern side of the island had existed in a state of 'stagnation' prior to its annexation by Haiti, Boyer commented in an 1827 speech that this made the region unable to profit fully from the benefits of industry. Because of this stagnation, the inhabitants would 'only attain by degrees the prosperity that is the fruit of liberty and independence', eventually benefiting both the Haitian state and themselves.[28] Boyer promised that the former slaves of Santo Domingo would gradually be integrated into the national community of a free and independent Haiti, through work and through an industrious contribution to the prosperity of the Haitian state.

The problematic nature of work in the nineteenth-century Caribbean — who should work, for whose profit, and to what end? — is conveyed in early Haitian writings via a number of contradictory messages. The underlying, difficult question to be asked is: does work still promote the freedom of the entire national community if the community is large, divergent and marked by deep inequalities? How far did the 'collective good' rhetorically evoked by Boyer and other Haitian politicians stretch, and where were the boundaries of this collectivity situated? The measure of how uncomfortable these questions were can be seen, I would argue, in the fascination of the island's literary elite with a myth of 'workless' indigenous communities as an idealized counter-narrative to the promotion of agricultural labour as the source of freedom for all. Far from the harsh limitations of militarized national agriculture and the *Rural Code*, nineteenth-century writings created the image of pre-colonial Haiti as a rural paradise. They were influenced by external, exoticizing perspectives on the tropics, as well as by a nationally shaped desire for a harmonious community or 'Concorde Intérieure' — a sentimentalized 'lost community' to cite Nancy, a fraternal idyll where no one had to be forced to work.[29]

Worklessness and the 'lost community': Resituating Haiti's Amerindian Past

In the epilogue to his *Haitian Revolutionary Studies*, Geggus has shown that the nascent concept of the Haitian nation was located not only in race (famously, article 14 of the 1805 Constitution proclaimed the entire population of the country 'under the generic denomination of blacks') and in opposition to French colonial brutality, but also in the continuous history of a territory and the choice of an Amerindian name, Haiti ('mountainous land'). As Geggus points out, this choice raises questions of 'ethnicity, memory and identity among the former slaves and free coloreds who created Haiti', and suggests a symbolic 'revalorization of Amerindian culture' of which independent Haiti was an early, nationalist example.[30] This process of renaming looks not only inward to the national community and its reassessed values, but also outward, sending a message to the rest of the Americas.

The enduring image of the mountains, or *mornes*, present within the name of Haiti is rooted in national memory and identity. Described by Beaubrun Ardouin in his *Geography of the Island of Haiti* as 'the boulevard of freedom and national independence', the *mornes* are associated with the guerrilla tactics of the Haitian revolutionaries, the fugitive slaves escaping the plantations, as well as Taino people seeking to evade or organize against the Spanish conquistadors.[31] The national myth of origins of the lost indigenous population is present in much of the nineteenth-century literary production of the Haitian and Dominican elite. In the poetic *History of the Caciques of Haiti* by Émile Nau, written in the 1830s, the Amerindian past is brought into the present and staged as a triumphant return and reestablishment of national sovereignty, as the entire island is wrested from the French and Spanish, and 'Saint Domingue becomes Haiti again'.[32] Nau stresses images of fraternity, historical continuity and exchange between the different populations of Haiti and a community of suffering under colonial rule: 'The African and the Indian held each other's hands in their chains' (14). In the work of nineteenth-century writers such as Vastey, Ardouin and Nau, Haiti's indigenous past is conceived as a spiritual inheritance, a kinship between colonized peoples in opposition to European colonial claims on the territorial space. 'As we inherited the chains of their servitude, so we inherited their homeland' (iv), Nau writes.

In Nau's *History*, that homeland is described as an Edenic, mythical place: 'The virginal and new island, on the first day of creation. Its soil bore no imprint of the hand of man' (49). This land is uncultivated — 'No fields were sown, either on the plains or on the slopes of the mountains, which even in the least civilized of countries, announces that the inhabitants cultivate the land' — and peaceful — 'everywhere that silence which testifies to the absence of human life or activity' (50). The agricultural activity described is subsistence-based, fruitful, rooted in the traditions of the land and unmarred by even the slightest force or effort:

The first Haitians, washed ashore in a great and magnificent land, had an abundance of venison and the products of the land and sea (. . .). They planted corn, yams, manioc and sweet potatoes, trusting their seed and vines to barely-traced furrows, and after a few months, they harvested corn cobs and huge, bulbous root vegetables that fed them. (52–3)

Nau refers to a myth of origins among the indigenous people of the island, based on the memory of how this simple subsistence agriculture had come into being. A large garden of yams, manioc, corn and sweet potatoes had been planted by a wise old man who, on his death, left the garden uncultivated. Years later, a group of Taino people found the garden and encountered his ghost: 'Appearing in the form of an old man, he taught them to plant, to harvest and to make their food' (57). In this myth of origins, everything is granted by Providence: the fertility and abundance of the land, and the good food grown in the Caribbean garden. According to a Haitian school primer from the same period, the indigenous people of the island were 'gentle, pacific and hospitable, with no cares and no needs', thanks to this miraculous generosity and the 'inexhaustible riches' of the land.[33] Peace, within and without, is a fundamental part of this mythical construction of a 'workless' community. The peaceful, gentle, subsistence agriculture image of the national community emerges, functioning as a manifestation of the contradiction between the national image of a land of freedom and the reality of state-imposed labour. This fantasized Haiti, tranquil and timeless, where the land provides freely and no work is needed, exposes the deep contradictions in the Haitian national self-image and the problematic imagining of a diverse and conflict-ridden national community.

Geggus and Largey have both suggested that the nineteenth-century interest in Haiti's indigenous past reflected the attempts of the elite to create an alternative racial lineage that minimized the influence of African culture, ancestry and belief systems whilst still rejecting European colonial dominance, by recognizing 'powerful symbolic ancestors' in the pre-Columbian inhabitants of the island, and forming 'a regal line that was derived from neither Europe nor Africa'.[34] Nau's *Histoire des Caciques* certainly attempts to create 'symbolic ancestors' for Haiti in the Taino people, although it does retain a clear sense of symbolic solidarity between the 'African' and the 'Indian' populations.

The projected 'confraternity of suffering' between the two groups is conceived both in terms of spiritual inheritance and a political solidarity born out of adversity, uniting two ethnically, socially and historically different communities against a common enemy. As such, it can be read as a tacit commentary on the bitter disputes over land and power in the nineteenth century, a period that saw Haiti's 'inheritance' contested among the black and mixed-race populations. While Boyer's Haitian state was extolling the virtues of work as a means of creating future national unity across the island, Nau and other writers were looking nostalgically to a pre-agricultural, 'workless' community of the mythologized past. This interpretation of Haiti's Amerindian heritage allows us to approach the community ideal from a different perspective, situating it within the debate over legitimacy, race, belonging and land ownership that marked the new nation from the outset.

In contrast with the State-defined rhetoric of 'Concordia' through labour, the myth of a lost community 'woven of tight, harmonious and infrangible bonds', characterized by a sense of 'organic communion' between its members, a 'fair distribution of tasks' and a 'happy equilibrium', spoke to the intellectual elite of Haiti at the time.[35] The production of national community as work and through work — an inherently flawed idea in itself, according to Nancy — was thus challenged in Haitian intellectual life during this period by a fantasy indigenous, workless community, a vision of peaceful inheritance passed down from one generation to the next. Yet this vision, ironically enough, found its closest nineteenth-century expression in the *Lakou* or African rural compounds, whose very existence was threatened by the *Rural Code*. While Haitian intellectuals like Émile Nau failed to draw any kind of parallel between the Amerindian past and the African-born rural populace in their writings, the subsistence agriculture, multi-generational family life and ancestral worship practices of the *Lakou* were far closer to the dream of indigenous 'lost community' in Nau's writing than the State-enforced nationalized and militarized agricultural regime of the national government. Ultimately, both fantasies of nineteenth-century community — the nationalized rhetoric of 'Concordia' and the lost Amerindian idyll of the liberal elite — lost ground when faced with the reality of the *moun andeyo*, the so-called 'outsiders' or others, whose successful counter-strategy of small plots of family or community land centred around the *Lakou* ultimately prevailed in rural, nineteenth-century Haiti.

NOTES

1 Victor Schœlcher, *Colonies étrangères et Haïti: Résultats de l'émancipation anglaise* (Paris: Pagnerre, 1843), II, 263; translations are mine, unless indicated otherwise.

2 Schœlcher, *Des colonies françaises, abolition immédiate de l'esclavage* (Paris: Pagnerre, 1842), xv.

3 The indigeneity of Dessalines and his soldiers is described by Jenson as both a 'paradoxical' and a 'traumatic indigeneity', referencing both a lost homeland (Africa) and a lost people (the Taino); Deborah Jenson, *Beyond the Slave Narrative: Politics, Sex and Manuscripts in the Haitian Revolution* (Liverpool: Liverpool University Press, 2011), 232.

4 Speech by Dessalines, cited in Thomas Madiou, *Histoire d'Haïti* (Port-au-Prince: J. Courtois, 1847–48), III, 48.

5 Madiou, *Histoire d'Haïti*, III, 48. On Lamour Dérance, Madiou notes that his soldiers were not organized in European military-style formation, instead they were 'divided by tribes, (...) Congos, Aradas, Ibos, Nabos, Mandingoes, Hausas' (Madiou, *Histoire d'Haïti*, III, 33).

6 'The Haitian Declaration of Independence (1 January 1804)' in *The Declaration of Independence: A Global History*, edited by David Armitage (Cambridge, MA: Harvard University Press, 2007), 193–8 (197). The moment of the two warring factions coming together to defeat the French at the symbolic heart of Haitian independence is depicted in the painting *Le Serment des Ancêtres* ('The Oath of the Ancestors', 1822). On early iconography of the revolution and the unifying symbolism of this painting, see Carlo Celius, 'Neoclassicism and the Haitian Revolution' in *The World of the Haitian Revolution*, edited by David Geggus and Norman Fiering (Bloomington: Indiana University Press, 2009), 352–92.

7 *La Concorde* 2 (20 May 1821), 7.

8 Jean-Pierre Boyer, 'Proclamation du gouvernement d'Haïti au peuple et à l'armée' in *Annuaire historique universel pour 1825*, edited by Charles-Louis Lesur (Paris: Chez A. Thoisnier-Desplaces, 1826), appendix, 146.

9 On the negotiation of Haiti's debt contracted to France in 1825, see David Nicholls, 'Haiti: Race, Slavery and Independence, 1804–1825' in *Slavery and Other Forms of Unfree Labour*, edited by Léonie J. Archer (London: Routledge, 1988), 225–38, and chapters by Blancpain, 'L'ordonnance de 1825 et la question de l'indemnité' and Gaillard-Pourchet, 'Aspects politiques et commerciaux de l'indemnisation haïtienne' in *Rétablissement de l'esclavage dans les colonies françaises: Aux origines d'Haïti*, edited by Yves Benot and Marcel Dorigny (Paris: Maisonneuve & Larose, 2003) 221–30 and 231–8.

10 See David Nicholls, *From Dessalines to Duvalier* (London: Macmillan, 1979); *Haïti: première république noire*, edited by Marcel Dorigny (Saint-Denis: SFHOM, 2007); Jean Casimir, *Haïti et ses élites: L'interminable dialogue de sourds* (Port-au-Prince: Editions de l'Université d'Etat d'Haïti, 2009).

11 Carolyn Fick, *The Making of Haiti: The Saint Domingue Revolution from Below* (Knoxville: University of Tennessee Press, 1990), 236.

12 Celia Britton, *The Sense of Community in French Caribbean Fiction* (Liverpool: Liverpool University Press, 2008), 2.

13 *The Concept of Community*, edited by David Minar and Scott Greer (London: Butterworth, 1969), 127.

14 Benedict Anderson, *Imagined Communities* (London: Verso, 2006 [1983]), 4.

15 Jean-Luc Nancy, 'La Comparution/The Compearance: From the Existence of "Communism" to the Community of "Existence"', *Political Theory* 20:3 (August 1992), 371–98 (386).

16 Jenson, *Beyond the Slave Narrative*, 122–60.

17 Pompée de Vastey, *Réflexions sur une lettre de Mazères, ex-Colon français, adressée à M. J. C. L. Sismonde de Sismondi, sur les Noirs et les Blancs, la Civilisation de l'Afrique, le Royaume d'Hayti, etc.* (Cap Henry: Chez P. Roux, 1816), 84.

18 *Gazette Royale d'Hayti*, 24 May 1816 (microfilm archives of the Bibliothèque nationale de France, M18400 (2)).

19 Nancy, 'La Comparution/The Compearance', 392.

20 Madiou, *Histoire d'Haïti*, I, i. David Nicholls has described the nineteenth-century version of national history as the 'mulatto legend', as it focused on revolutionaries like Ogé, Chavannes, Rigaud and Pétion who were part of the light-skinned elite (*From Dessalines to Duvalier*, 67).

21 Laurent Dubois, *Haiti: The Aftershocks of History* (New York: Metropolitan Books, 2012), 104.

22 Gérard Barthélemy, 'Aux origines d'Haïti : "Africains" et paysans' in *Haïti: première république noire*, 103–20 (113). See also Michel-Rolph Trouillot, *Haiti, State Against Nation* (New York: Monthly Review Press, 1990) and Mimi Sheller, *Democracy After Slavery: Black Publics and Peasant Radicalism in Haiti and Jamaica* (Gainesville: University Press of Florida, 2000).

23 Vastey, *Réflexions politiques sur quelques ouvrages et journaux français, concernant Hayti* (Sans Souci: Imprimerie Royale, 1817), 37.
24 Nicholls, 'Haiti: Race, Slavery and Independence', 231–2.
25 Boyer, 'Proclamation du gouvernement d'Haïti au peuple et à l'armée', 146.
26 'Code Rural' article 3, in *Six Codes d'Haïti* (Port-au-Prince: C. Descouriet, 1828), 66196 (661) http://ufdc.ufl.edu/AA00000664/00001/, consulted 31 December 2012.
27 'Code Rural' article 4, in *Six Codes d'Haïti*, 662.
28 'Message from the President of Haiti to the Chamber of Representatives, Port-au-Prince, 28 April 1827' in *Recueil général des lois et actes du gouvernement d'Haïti, tome V*, edited by Linstant Pradine (Paris: Auguste Durand, 1866), 44–5. http://ufdc.ufl.edu/UF00074014/00002/, consulted 31 December 2012.
29 Jean-Luc Nancy, *The Inoperative Community*, edited by Peter Connor (Minneapolis: University of Minnesota Press, 1991), 9.
30 David Geggus, 'Epilogue' in *Haitian Revolutionary Studies* (Bloomington: Indiana University Press, 2002), 205–20 (205).
31 Beaubrun Ardouin, *Géographie de l'île d'Haïti, précédée du précis et de la date des événemens les plus remarquables de son histoire* (Port-au-Prince, 1832), 58. Vastey also described the *mornes* of Haiti as the national heartland of resistance to colonial rule, referring for example to the *Baoruco* mountains where Cacique Henri fought the Spanish: *Le Système colonial dévoilé* (Cap Henry: P. Roux, 1814), 3–12.
32 Émile Nau, *Histoire des Caciques d'Haïti* (Port-au-Prince: T. Bouchereau, 1855), 11; subsequent references in the text. Nau's book was first published in serial form in *L'Union* between 1837 and 1839 (Léon-François Hoffmann, 'L'Élément indien dans la conscience collective des Haïtiens', *Études Créoles* XVII:1 (1994), 11–38).
33 *Alphabet à l'usage de la jeunesse haïtienne, suivi d'un résumé de la géographie, de l'histoire et de la chronologie de l'île d'Haïti jusqu'en 1859* (Paris: Émile Mellier, 1859), 33.
34 Michael Largey, *Vodou Nation: Haitian Art Music and Cultural Nationalism* (Chicago: University of Chicago Press, 2006), 128. Geggus, *Haitian Revolutionary Studies*, 218.
35 Nancy, *The Inoperative Community*, 9.

Community in Post-earthquake Writing from Haiti

Martin Munro

Abstract:
This article develops Celia Britton's insights into community in French Caribbean writing in two ways. First, it considers Jacques Roumain's *Gouverneurs de la rosée* and its image of community in the broader context of modern and contemporary Haitian fiction; and second it discusses representations of community in two Haitian works written after the earthquake of 2010, an event that literally destroyed many communities and has forced Haitian authors to rethink relationships between different groups in Haiti and between human life, the cities, nature and the land.

Keywords: Haiti, Caribbean, community, earthquake, literature, Roumain, Laferrière, Saint-Eloi

In her 2008 book, *The Sense of Community in French Caribbean Fiction*, Celia Britton writes of Jacques Roumain's *Gouverneurs de la rosée*, proposing that the novel is one in which 'the theme of community is central'.[1] Through careful analysis of the novel, she argues convincingly that it embodies an ideal of organic community which is largely compatible with Jean-Luc Nancy's theory of common being, the version of an immanent community which, as Britton glosses, is 'characterized by a fusional unity in which all its members identify with the community as collective subject, and this identification is continually reinforced by cultural forms which reflect back to the members images of their unity' (9). As Britton shows, again drawing on Nancy, the notion of common being is a 'phantasy that is always situated in the past and that has always already been lost to dissension' (21). In Roumain's novel, the unified community of the past is evoked through the memory of the 'coumbite,' the communal work system

Paragraph 37.2 (2014): 193–204
DOI: 10.3366/para.2014.0121
© Edinburgh University Press
www.euppublishing.com/para

that existed before the village of Fonds-Rouge split due to a family feud. The returning exile saviour figure Manuel charges himself with the task of restoring the lost communal unity. His project seeks to re-create 'lost intimacy and communion,' and is, as Britton recognizes, 'essentially nostalgic' (21). One of the most revealing and original insights that Britton offers into this much-read novel is that its great success can be in large part attributed to the image it presents of the 'perfect community' (23). 'The novel's power', Britton writes, 'is intimately dependent on its evocation of common being', and 'its ability to move us depends on the way the text *produces* the community by means of a very carefully orchestrated system of repeated and interconnected elements' (23). As Britton argues, *Gouverneurs de la rosée* is to a great degree characterized by 'closure, unity and consistency', and Roumain's intention in the novel is apparently to 'eliminate difference and contradiction' (28).

This article develops Britton's insights into community in French Caribbean writing in two ways. First, it considers *Gouverneurs de la rosée* and its image of community in the broader context of modern and contemporary Haitian fiction; and second, it discusses representations of community in two Haitian works written after the earthquake of 2010, an event that literally destroyed many communities and has forced Haitian authors to rethink relationships between different groups in Haiti and between human life, the cities, nature and the land.

The first point to make about *Gouverneurs de la rosée* is that, despite its reputation as the quintessential Haitian novel, it is a quite unique work in the history of modern and contemporary Haitian fiction. It is difficult to think of another work that presents its community in such a closed, unified way. Perhaps the work that comes closest to Roumain's vision of the organic Haitian peasant community is Jacques-Stephen Alexis's *Compère Général Soleil* (1955). In this, Alexis's first novel, the hinterland is idealized in ways that recall *Gouverneurs de la rosée*; in both cases the countryside retains connotations of resistance, cultural roots, and of individual and collective freedom. The city, conversely, is presented as a place of exile and alienation, far removed from the 'authentic' countryside. If the city is considered to be a less authentic space, it is because, as Michael Dash says, '[i]t is in the city that the Caribbean's encounter with modernity is most evident', and its mean-ings and conflicts are 'opposed to pastoral zones of timeless seclusion'.[2]

Alexis's second novel, *Les Arbres musiciens* largely shares with his first its idealized image of peasant culture and the rural community. By contrast, Alexis's third novel *L'Espace d'un cillement*, published in 1959, is the author's most urbanized work, and its characters are the most detached from the country and from its associated concepts of original, untainted culture and unified community. Given that neither of its two central characters originate in Haiti (they are Cuban), the novel represents a step away from the preoccupation with rural authenticity and towards a reappraisal of urban space. Urban living in the novel provides a commonality of experience and a sense of community for the Caribbean wanderer, an immediate and accessible sense of belonging, quite different to the more closed idea of 'authentic' rural identity, in that the latter relies on lineage, enracination and stasis. In effect Alexis's final novel introduces to Haitian literature many of the exile-related themes that will come to dominate the post-war period, a time in which the Haitian novel distances itself from indigenism and Roumain and reworks its idea of community.

It seems significant too that Alexis's movement away from the Roumain-inspired, idealized vision of community and towards a more splintered, urban, exilic notion of community and culture should occur just as Haiti slid into dictatorship. The dystopian society that the 29-year-long Duvalier dictatorships created effectively ended Roumain's and Alexis's idealized visions of community, and from this point authors have tended to present communities characterized by unbridgeable divisions, fear and violence. In Nancy's terms, this shift in Haitian writing marks a movement away from myth, which has to do with 'totality, completion, and *constructing* an identity' to literature, which is related to 'the fragmentary, the incomplete, the suspension rather than the institution of meanings'. As Britton argues, literature in Nancy's terms 'does not communicate *a* meaning, but "unworks" meaning in general' (14).

The meanings that the most prominent works of post-Roumain Haitian literature 'unwork' relate primarily to the ideas on culture and community propagated by the nationalist-indigenist movement that was founded during the American occupation of 1915–1934. In Lyonel Trouillot's *Street of Lost Footsteps* (1998), an elderly madam declares that Haitian history is a 'corset, a stifling cell (...) an apocalyptic calypso', and that Haiti is an 'epic failure factory (...) an abyss for tightrope walkers'.[3] Everything, she says, began 'with the wind', with gusts of 'folkloric-tropical-negritudinal rubbish' (3). In other words, according to this narrator, the roots of the dystopian present lie in the utopian myths of the indigenists and nationalists, and the myth not only misrepresents reality but contributes to its degradation, creating an illusory idea of community and togetherness while in truth the society is falling apart.

Thirty years before Trouillot, Marie Vieux-Chauvet offered perhaps the most striking and powerful literary counterpoint to the comforting myths of the indigenists in her classic trilogy *Amour, Colère, Folie*.[4] In each of these novels, the community is radically divided, chiefly along class and colour lines. In *Amour*, the narrator Claire's alienation is determined largely by the dark shade of her skin; her two sisters are light-skinned, but Claire is 'stained' by darkness, 'the surprise that mixed blood held for our parents' (12). In her insular middle-class milieu, Claire's dark skin is a source of disavowed shame for her family, and her life is lived almost exclusively within the walls of the family home. Claire is doubly alienated in that her dark skin sets her apart from the light-skinned bourgeoisie and conversely her middle-class background differentiates her from the dark-skinned lower classes. There is therefore little sense of community at all, and life is lived indoors, locked inside individual rooms, alone with one's fears and frustrations. Chauvet's fundamental question, indeed the fundamental question of so many post-Roumain Haitian novels, is put by the Frenchman Jean Luze, who asks: 'This hatred you have for each other, where does it come from?' (56). The modern Haitian novel in this way often counteracts the nationalist rhetoric of racial and national plenitude. If indigenism had sought to valorize the idea of the 'Haitian soul', Chauvet suggests the radical alienation and emptiness ultimately created by racial rhetoric in her character Claire who is a 'body without soul' (82–3).

Chauvet's dystopian view of community has proven to be highly influential, far more so than Roumain's mythical version. One can trace Chauvet's influence to varying degrees in virtually all Haitian fiction published after her trilogy, most recently in Kettly Mars's 2010 novel *Saisons sauvages*, which is essentially a contemporary reworking of Chauvet's *Amour*.[5] Mars's work is the story of a middle-class mulatto woman, Nirvah Leroy, whose husband is arrested by the Duvalierist authorities for engaging in left-wing political activity. Nirvah visits the Secretary of State for Public Security to ask for news of her husband, but in order to ensure her family's survival, she becomes the minister's lover, a situation that is humiliating and demeaning but also affords her a certain prestige in the society ruled by the Duvalier dictatorship. It is the ambivalent position of the woman that Mars explores in a novel that revisits the unhealed wounds of dictatorship and the ever relevant themes memorably evoked by Chauvet. In Mars's novel, just as in Chauvet's, it is the situation of the woman in, or rather apart from, her community that is highlighted. There seems to be a subtle political analogy developed through Nirvah's entrapment by the *noiriste* minister. Most apparently, the forced–desired relationship suggests some of the historical complexities of class and colour relations in Haiti. More precisely, Vincent takes possession of Nirvah just as Duvalier is perfecting his complete control of Haiti, destroying all opposition, and naming himself President for Life. The two acts seem closely related; the invasion of Nirvah's private space and her body is synchronous with the omnipresence of the macoutes, who themselves 'infiltrate' every area of Haitian life. The minister's statement to her that he will not harm her 'as long as you do not make me do so' is a loaded promise that echoes the broader tactic of confusing paternalistic offers of protection with threats of violent retribution (134). Nirvah seems to be aware of the close relationship between the two projects when she remarks that there is no hope, that 'the roots of dictatorship sink deeper every day into the land of Haiti' while at the same time Vincent is about to 'achieve his deepest fantasy, to dominate and possess a mulatto woman' (135). Ultimately the situation becomes unbearable for Nirvah and she flees Port-au-Prince attempting to reach the Dominican Republic.

Mars thus raises the question of exile, a key issue that has shaped Haitian authors' views on community, especially since the beginning of the Duvalier era and the forced departures of many of Haiti's intellectuals. Exile quite obviously further complicates the idea of community, and in many works of exile the individual is often presented as radically alone, separated from home and community and struggling to create any sense of community and togetherness in the place of exile. On the other hand, when the exile returns to Haiti, he or she has difficulty in reconnecting with the community they left behind and which has developed in its own idiosyncratic ways in the absence of the exile. There is much more to say on the theme of exile and community, but I want to focus in the final part of this article on the idea of community as presented in two works written after the earthquake of 12 January 2010. In particular, I will concentrate on the ways in which two prominent authors have re-invoked the theme of nature and its relationship to community.

Post-earthquake Writing and Community

In Lyonel Trouillot's 2009 novel *Yanvalou pour Charlie* one character remarks that 'to construct, one must destroy'.[6] Will meaningful reconstruction result from the terrible destruction brought about by the earthquake? While it is difficult to be overly optimistic in this regard, reading some of the early post-earthquake works produced by key Haitian authors, one can sense that the event quite literally shook the foundations of the community, or rather, the diverse and divided communities that made up the Haitian society critiqued by Chauvet, Mars, Trouillot and others. What is fascinating too is that in several of these works, the reworked notions of community reincorporate nature as a fundamental element, and in a sense reactivate some of the imagery associated with the indigenists, Roumain and *Gouverneurs de la rosée*. What do these returns to nature mean for our understanding of community in Haiti?

One of the first works to be published following the earthquake was Dany Laferrière's chronicle *Tout bouge autour de moi*.[7] The very title evokes an image of the author at the centre of a still shifting world, in which he stands shaken and alone. Typically, he insists on the *moi*; as an exiled author his works are generally concerned with his own personal fate and arguably less interested in the notion of community. One gets the sense that he wants to resist being redirected, thrown off the singular literary and intellectual path that he has carefully shaped for himself for over a quarter of a century. At the same time, however, he does feel an obligation to speak for Haiti in the post-earthquake world. And in this sense, he is drawn into a communal space that he has previously tended to avoid. Laferrière's sense of community is founded on culture, which is he says, 'the only thing that can stand up to the earthquake'. 'Art, to me,' he says, 'is not a luxury, it structures our life and proves itself to be as necessary as bread' (72). The cultural community he speaks of is constituted by not only the literary and intellectual culture, but also the culture of the people, that which structures and gives meaning to their lives (8). Now is not the time for tears, he says, but to 'carry on down our path' (8). The switch to the collective possessive form 'our' is significant; in the book he is increasingly drawn from the singular to the collective, and ties his own fate as never before to that of the people and the nation.

Although he details the destruction brought about by the earthquake, Laferrière is sensitive to the ways in which it has not destroyed everything. The earthquake 'attacked' all that was apparently strong and solid—concrete structures that crumbled in an instant (31). Curiously, some of the most apparently delicate and frail objects— babies, flowers growing in the hotel garden—survived, and proved themselves more enduring than the concrete buildings (31). There is a muted suggestion here that in mercilessly tearing down the apparently solid, man-made objects the earthquake has also exposed, however fleetingly, the underlying strength and enduring qualities of natural phenomena.[8] Included among these natural phenomena are the people of Port-au-Prince themselves. The people are aligned with the enduring flowers in the author's observation that the disaster has brought before the 'bedazzled' eyes of the world 'a people that gangrenous institutions do not allow to blossom' (40). Just as the perfume and the visual beauty of flowers survive, Laferrière suggests, so the deep humanity of a constrained and mistreated people persists and proves itself imperishable in the face of the disaster. Also, as if to emphasize the point, Laferrière refers to the human survivors as 'a *forest* of remarkable people' (41, my italics). The idea that the people's endurance is the result of natural and not societal phenomena is further suggested in the first image he recalls after leaving the hotel, of a woman selling mangoes by the roadside. Struck by the woman's courage, he reflects that 'these people have never received anything from the State', and seems to imply that their best hope lies in this kind of agrarian self-sufficiency, which in turn carries echoes of the traditional *lakou* system of land ownership (47). Instituted in the early post-revolutionary period, the *lakou* was a profoundly egalitarian system set up to counter the state's attempts to re-impose a plantation economy and 'emphasized self-reliance through working the soil'.[9] In Laferrière's text, the mangoes, like the woman, have survived, and appear to offer the woman her best (indeed, only) chance of continued existence, through agrarian self-reliance.

Laferrière also suggests a renewed personal bond with the country in writing that on the first night, sleeping under the stars, he was 'at one' (*fait corps*) with the land. This echoes directly a remark he makes in the book about Frankétienne's relationship with Port-au-Prince, and implies that the earthquake has brought him into a newly intimate bond with Haiti. It also, more indirectly, seems to echo the idea of an intimate relationship to the land that is so important to *Gouverneurs de la rosée*.

But this is not a work of nostalgia, and the future Laferrière foresees is far from that critiqued by Britton in Roumain's novel as 'a repetition of the past, a closed space which confers a shared identity on all the people within it in opposition to the outside' (28). There is no circular chronology in Laferrière's vision of the future; instead he predicts difference, change and modernization. He believes the rich to be the least in favour of modernization, which requires a degree of sharing and the recognition that the country shares a collective destiny (115). The challenge will be, he says, to create a country from a collection of individuals (115). In other words, Laferrière foregrounds the importance of community building to Haiti's immediate and long-term future. And while the earthquake reawakens in him an interest in themes of nature and strengthens his bond with the land, he stops well short of offering a Roumain-like idealized vision of nation and community. He finally insists that complete harmony is an unrealistic, even undesired goal, for as he says, again using a natural metaphor, 'life is this river that carries everything, the mud as much as the clear water' (116).

Laferrière's experience of the earthquake was shared with Rodney Saint-Eloi; it was only when Laferrière finally left for Montreal that the two were separated. Saint-Eloi's account of the earthquake, *Haïti kenbe la!* (Haiti hold on!), thus offers an opportunity to compare two versions of the same events, and presents some revealing contrasts in narrative form and subjective experience.[10] In terms of Saint-Eloi's vision of nature and community, too, there are some telling similarities.

Like Laferrière, Saint-Eloi notices that amidst the human devastation, plants and flowers have remained largely untouched. The lilac flowers in particular evoke memories of childhood, of a time that now appears carefree and distant, its everyday normality as irrecoverable as the past time (132–3). The lilacs serve as a reminder of that time, but also that nature survives and is durable in a way that humans and their creations are not. Like Laferrière, too, Saint-Eloi suggests that the earthquake calls for a renewed relationship with nature, a move away from the hyper-urban world and a respect for nature that has proven its resilience and strength amidst the devastation. Tellingly, the living are described as being upright like flamboyant trees (178). Importantly, too, nature's persistence and its inbuilt impulse for survival and rebirth implicitly counters the human discourse of apocalypse and fatalism that Saint-Eloi talks of elsewhere in the book, and which seems to welcome death as an affirmation, and even to will that death to come. The scene that Saint-Eloi depicts of flowers and plants alive and growing still in the midst of the human and material devastation suggests the fallacy of apocalyptic thought and the limitations of human intelligence when it is focused solely on human destiny, and when it believes the human can be separated from the rest of the natural world.

The qualities attributed to nature of endurance and renewal are subtly connected to literature in Saint-Eloi's presentation of a young woman, sitting by the hotel reading a book in the shadow of a palm tree, wearing a blue flowery dress and with a yellow hibiscus in her hair (148). Immediately preceding this scene, he had wondered about the role of literature and stated that it should serve something more than the 'little ego fairs' that literary festivals sometimes amount to (147). The image of the young woman lost in reading suggests that through books one can attain a consciousness that at once takes the reader out of the moment and connects her intimately to it. The flowers on her dress and in her hair, moreover, make a connexion between the woman, reading and nature, as if to suggest that the three are complementary, and that books are themselves part of nature, or at least a means by which one can connect with nature through 'culture', and are part of the means of survival and revitalizing existence.[11]

Visual art is similarly seen as a vital means of incorporating the memories of the event into the consciousness of the traumatized individual, and by extension the community. Meeting an artist called Michel, who had survived two days trapped under debris, Saint-Eloi reflects on how to relate the story of the earthquake and the ways in which it will manifest itself in the mind of the artist. 'What colour will he dream in?' he asks, 'What elusive lines will inhabit the canvas? Will the earth be like a solid colour with no horizon?' (164). The artist will now have an 'essential vision' of things and will not be able to paint in the way he did before. Painting will be the only thing that will help him carry on and treat the wounds left by the earthquake. Words, the author says, make the weight of the earth easier to bear, while with colours, he wonders whether a storm can be transformed into a rainbow (164). Again, as with the woman reading, art is related to the restorative powers of nature, and is indeed seen as a part of the natural world itself.

In contrast to the enduring natural phenomena, the most conspicuous of monuments to human power and political ambition, the National Palace, is fatally damaged by the earthquake. Every Haitian, Saint-Eloi says, dreams of reaching the Palace, the house of the people that is nonetheless jealously guarded by the elite (165). The history of every citizen begins and ends with the Palace, which is a 'white monster that dominates the town and the soul' (167) and the edifice onto which are projected the hopes, fears, and fantasies of the people. Saint-Eloi and the people he encounters seem to have ambiguous feelings about the demise of the Palace; on the one hand it was the most visible national landmark, and on the other it symbolized political ambition and the absolute superiority of the ruling classes.

The phenomena that the earthquake seems to have exposed and attacked most directly are human folly and vanity, underpinned by the segregated class system and the survival of the 'colonial mindset' (228); and it is difficult in this regard not to read the image of the collapsed National Palace as a sign of a form of natural justice imposing itself.

As a natural phenomenon the earthquake has no conscience, in that it is inevitably indifferent to human folly.[12] And yet its effects were particularly concentrated on areas in which that folly was most prevalent — the Palace and its associations with the vanities of the elite; the city slums, the results of ill-advised urbanization and class segregation. The earthquake has in a sense a narrative, a story that can be constructed through reading its many diverse and often paradoxical effects. One of the most prevalent strands of this narrative relates to the unsustainable nature of previous social relations, which itself is connected to the idea that the various social groups share a fundamentally common destiny, that no single group can live any longer in isolation from the rest. This idea is implied in Saint-Eloi's thoughts on the nature of living in Haiti, and indeed on whether Haiti and its people can be said to exist: does the verb 'to exist' have the same weight, he asks, in Haiti as it does in London? The author's reflections are provoked by his consideration of the concept of resilience, a quality often attributed to the Haitian people, especially in times of crisis. Arguing that resilience is a concept that 'enchants' intellectuals, to the point that they forget the 'beings of flesh and blood' and the suffering that 'eats away at our insides', he finds that it signifies that 'we are already dead, but are still standing upright through habit' (259). As such, he suggests that the phenomenon of existing suspended between life and death is not confined to the poorest or to the criminal gangs, but is common to all classes, connecting them and tying their fates in an intimate bond that means that no single group can truly thrive and live while others remain forgotten, living on the fault-line between living and dying, and between the past, the present and the future of Haiti.

From these brief discussions of two post-earthquake works, we can sense that community is and will remain a key issue in Haitian writing for a long time to come. This is because, for many Haitian authors, the earthquake marked a radical rupture with time and history. The earthquake seems to some extent to have ended a 200-year-long period in which history has turned in circles and repetitions. Jacques Roumain's response to an entrenched history of social division was to evoke an ideal image of the past and to view the future as a harmonious repetition of the past. While Alexis shared with Roumain an idealized conception of the hinterland and peasant culture, he also was aware of the ways in which dictatorship and exile were rendering such models of culture and community increasingly obsolete. Authors such as Chauvet, Trouillot, Mars, Laferrière and many others in effect wrote against Roumain's indigenist-nationalist notions of community and evoked a dystopian community, characterized by apparently irreconcilable differences. But their time may have come to an end too. Just as these authors and the events they wrote about superseded Roumain, so they themselves have in some senses been superseded by the earthquake, and now face a new reality that will require new models, new visions of society, culture and community. One of the most interesting cultural developments of the post-earthquake period has been the coming to prominence of a new, younger generation of authors, figures such as Marvin Victor, James Noël and Makenzy Orcel, writers born, in a sense, of the earthquake, and whose works contain some of the most compelling and urgent commentaries on post-earthquake existence.[13] Perhaps for the first time in Haiti's literary history, authors are now focused less on the past than the future, the time to come that will have to be different to that which has gone before. There is now no way back. And to adapt what Britton ultimately says about *Gouverneurs de la rosée*, the imperfections and 'incompleteness' of the previous versions of community provide 'an opening onto the outside world' and to the future that, however tragic this period is for the nation, makes this a quite 'exhilarating' time to write and read about Haiti (35).[14]

NOTES

1   Celia Britton, *The Sense of Community in French Caribbean Fiction* (Liverpool: Liverpool University Press, 2008), 19; subsequent references in the text.

2   J. Michael Dash, *The Other America: Caribbean Literature in a New World Context* (Charlottesville: University of Virginia Press, 1998), 8.

3   Lyonel Trouillot, *Street of Lost Footsteps*, translated by Linda Coverdale (Lincoln, NE: University of Nebraska Press, 2003), 1.

4   Marie Chauvet, *Amour, Colère, Folie* (Paris: Gallimard, 1968) ; all translations are mine unless indicated otherwise.

5   Kettly Mars, *Saisons sauvages* (Paris: Mercure de France, 2010).

6   Lyonel Trouillot, *Yanvalou pour Charlie* (Arles: Actes Sud, 2009), 120.

7   Dany Laferrière, *Tout bouge autour de moi* (Montreal: Mémoire d'encrier, 2010).

8   He notes later that birds 'do not seem concerned by the situation' (39). Also, he reflects that whereas hurricanes sometimes damage nature more than human life, '[e]arthquakes destroy that which man has patiently built while leaving the flower intact' (44).

9   Laurent Dubois, *Haiti, The Aftershocks of History* (New York: Metropolitan Books, 2012), 108.

10 Rodney Saint-Eloi, *Haïti kenbe la!* (Neuilly-sur-Seine: Michel Lafon, 2010).

11 He states later that it is 'stories that bring people together' (266).

12 This is not to say that human or divine characteristics have not been attributed to the earthquake by various sectors of Haitian society and indeed by foreign commentators, from religious groups to conspiracy theorists.

13 See, for example, Marvin Victor, *Corps mêlés* (Paris: Gallimard, 2011), Makenzy Orcel, *Les Immortelles* (Montreal: Mémoire d'encrier, 2011), and James Noël, *Kana Sutra* (La Roque d'Antheron: Vents d'Ailleurs, 2011).

14 On the ethical issues involved in writing about post-earthquake Haiti from the outside, see Paul Farmer, *Haiti After the Earthquake* (New York: Public Affairs, 2011), 1–5. Writing about Haitian literature no doubt raises its own ethical questions, though the process is slightly different in that a literary critic does not or should not 'speak for' the victims of disaster, but should engage openly with literary works that deal to varying degrees with the disaster, and which themselves often contain reflections on the ethics and general worth of writing in a time of disaster.

Working, Writing and the Antillean Postcolony: Patrick Chamoiseau and Gisèle Pineau

Lorna Milne

Abstract:

Patrick Chamoiseau's *Un Dimanche au cachot* (2007) and Gisèle Pineau's *Folie, aller simple* (2010) refer to the authors' professions (respectively social worker and nurse) to explore the tensions besetting Caribbean territories that belong integrally to the French Republic, yet are culturally distinct from the Hexagon. While both writers use a version of 'staged marginality' to raise questions about the 'imagined community' of the Republic, each adopts a different political approach and writing strategy. Chamoiseau appears still to struggle with binary colonial anxieties in relation to France, despite his professed immersion in Glissant's transcending 'Tout-Monde'; Pineau presents a less theorized, more integrative 'transcultural' Frenchness based on her personal experience. These contrasting interpretations highlight the need for a theoretical approach to the Antilles that accommodates both the shifting, relational dynamic associated with Glissant's postcolonial perspective, and the binary axis of centre and periphery more commonly associated with colonialism.

Keywords: Chamoiseau, Pineau, Antillean literature, postcolonial theory, imagined communities, transnational French Studies

Celia Britton's seminal *Edouard Glissant and Postcolonial Theory*[1] set the tone for much scholarly analysis of Antillean literature that was to follow, and Glissant himself is now an essential figure in postcolonial studies more generally, most quoted for his dynamic vision of *Tout-Monde*, a vast, chaotic 'whole-world' of becoming through exchanges and relations.[2] Indeed, since the Caribbean is quintessentially an area of exchange and encounter in its history, geography and cultures, many

Paragraph 37.2 (2014): 205–220
DOI: 10.3366/para.2014.0122
© Edinburgh University Press
www.euppublishing.com/para

writers and scholars have (assisted by Glissant) come to see wide-open flux, porosity and exchange as the key principles in theorizing the region.

Yet while his native Antilles are naturally bound up in Glissant's vision and can of course be conceptualized as free-floating relational entities within the theoretical *Tout-Monde*, Glissant's cosmopolitan perspective may tempt us to overlook the material reality of the islands themselves, reflected in Antillean cultural production of all kinds: Guadeloupe and Martinique are two of France's five *Départements et Régions d'Outre-Mer* (DROM), anchored in the formal political, social and economic structures of the Republic.[3] This fact complicates their status as 'postcolonies',[4] and calls for an analytical framework that takes special account of their particularities, most notably the peculiar tension between cultural distinctiveness and republican integration that besets the relation of the DROM to the French state. Discussing two texts that exemplify this unavoidable engagement with structures and ideas forged by metropolitan France through the professional activities of their narrators, this essay will consider the implications of these tensions for the 'imagined community'[5] of the French nation, and for our reading of the Antilles as elements of it.

Within three years of one another, Patrick Chamoiseau (Martinique) and Gisèle Pineau (Guadeloupe) published books containing remarkably similar elements, including extended reference to the jobs they do in addition to their careers as writers.[6] In Chamoiseau's novel, *Un dimanche au cachot*, the narrator is a youth social worker called Patrick Chamoiseau, as is the author himself. Pineau's 'récit' (narrative), *Folie, aller simple: journée ordinaire d'une infirmière*, discusses the author's work as a psychiatric nurse. Each text covers one day in its narrator's professional life in a single, closed location, far from 'normal' society: Patrick finds himself literally in a tight spot with a problem teenager; Gisèle is in a closed psychiatric ward.[7] From these positions of 'staged marginality',[8] both underline their status as 'ultramarins' (citizens of the Overseas Departments, *DC*, 22) while reflecting on the nature and conditions of their employment. At the same time, both explicitly refer to the fact that they are also creative writers.

In *Un Dimanche*, a single narrating 'je' (I) is multiplied by a play of *mises en abyme* across three diegeses, each of which blurs into the others.[9] In one of these, Patrick is called out on a rainy Sunday in his twin professional capacities of social worker and story-teller, to deal with Caroline, an abused teenager hiding in the ruins of a *cachot*—a small, stone-vaulted and low-lying prison cell on a former plantation. Once there, Patrick tells Caroline a story that is the second diegesis, set on the same plantation in the 1820s and taking up the bulk of the book. A third diegesis envelops the other two and outlines the writing of the book itself.

Early in the text, the third narrating 'je' explains that during the week, like his compatriots in the Overseas Departments, Patrick espouses the various 'figures' (22) imposed by society and citizenship for 'tout peuple livré aux dépendances' (23) (any people given over to dependency): consumer, subscriber, welfare beneficiary, amongst others. His time and identity are also structured by being a busy professional, and he goes along with the performance, wearing two distinct 'masques' (24) (masks). As a public figure, he takes part in debates, comments on the news and 'assume du mieux possible cette espèce d'"écrivain" que l'on a fait de moi' (23) (internalize, as best I can, this sort of 'writer' I've been turned into). Wearing his other mask, that of 'une sorte d'éducateur' (some kind of social worker), he equally acts a part; with his young delinquents, he says:

il me faut composer jour après jour de sincères pantomimes: croire au juste, à l'injuste, au Bien contre le Mal, à la solidarité, aux lois républicaines, au droit pénal, à la croissance, à l'Europe, au lien social, aux psychothérapies, aux stages merdiques et, bien entendu, à la réinsertion... (24).

(day after day I've got to put on a sincere pantomime-act: believing in what is fair, what is unfair, in Good against Evil, in supporting one another, in the laws of the Republic, in penal justice, in economic growth, in Europe, in social partnership, in psychotherapy, in crap training courses and, of course, in rehabilitation...)

'Staging' himself in this way, the narrator refutes the notion of a stable, easily defined self that might be summed up by national citizenship or profession, by using the vocabulary of play-acting, by referring deprecatingly to his roles (a 'sort of' writer, 'some kind of' social worker), and by deploying irony to suggest that a social worker has to fit into a whole French Republican ideological and cultural outlook he may find it difficult to share.

The play-acting stops on Sundays, however, when almost everything in Martinique closes down and the 'performance' of work is set aside: 'La scène perd ses décors. Le rideau tombe sans grâce' (The stage set vanishes. The curtain falls mercilessly) and 'Chacun est (...) en soi-même sous un oxygène devenu asphyxiant' (23) (Everyone is (...) left to himself, breathing oxygen that becomes suffocating). As days of rest,

Sundays, especially rainy ones, hold out no masks, and are accordingly described in terms of emptiness, formlessness and 'décentrement' (25) (decentredness). Patrick himself usually spends his Sundays writing, and finds that their absence of structure, augmented by the liquid shapelessness and 'disponibilité' (unconstraint) of flowing rainwaters, invites a dissolving or '*diffraction*' of the self into imagination, through which the writer (thus 'left to himself') inhabits the imaginary egos of his characters, and is 'explosé d'écriture' (25) (shattered by writing). This vocabulary of outward-looking freedom contrasts with the lexis of imprisonment that characterizes professional and public roles structured by others — in particular by the metropole that makes of Antilleans a 'people given over to dependency'. The third-diegesis narrator hints at his own sense of imprisonment, for example when he moves from the solitary experience of freedom through Sunday writing to the performance of his professional duty as writer and social worker as perceived by others: in his handling of Caroline, he notices a tendency to conform to type in both roles and confesses 'J'étais effaré de voir comment ces deux personnages me *maintenaient* jour après jour en pays convenu' (132, my emphasis) (I was alarmed to see how these two characters *kept* me day after day on conventional ground).

The suggestion of being locked in by particular roles (in this case, professional ones), sets up echoes with the figure of the physically imprisoning *cachot*. This in turn chimes with a metaphorical association that is established, also near the start of the book, between the *cachot*, an originary manifestation of actual imprisonment, and an important figure — also presented as foundational — of *mental* closure. This figurative closure is represented by reference to the notorious racial taxonomy of the Antillean population published by Moreau de Saint-Méry in 1797.[10] Describing Moreau somewhat dubiously as 'le premier à vivre l'énigme' (26) (the first to experience the enigma) of Creole identity, the narrator notes that Moreau's project begins with two distinct and supposedly 'pure' racial categories — 'un Blanc et une Négresse' (26) (a white man and a negress) — whose union produces the mixed-race 'Mulâtre' (mulatto). After the introduction of this third racial term (and soon a fourth, fifth and so on, as the number of possible miscegenations multiplies), Moreau provides a plethora of further labels, each based on the exact proportion of racial heritage in the corresponding category. Thus, instead of appreciating that each member of this riotously variegated population represents in her- or himself alone 'une globalisation soudaine, un ouvert déroutant' (27) (a sudden globalization, a disorientating openness), Moreau's absurd taxonomy shows that he 'demeura dans le cachot de son esprit' (28) (remained in the *cachot* of his own mind).

While Sunday stands for the possibility of unfettered liberty of the imagination, then, the *cachot* itself, and Moreau's *cachot* of a mind, are a composite metaphor for all kinds of enclosure: the judgemental jargon of social work; the conformity of the professional 'writer'; other masks proffered by society; the restricted space of a small island; limited ways of thinking; the past; the abuse that programmes Caroline's behaviour. The text suggests it is easy to succumb to the temptations of the *cachot*, especially for the 'people given over to dependency' of the DROM for whom the unaccustomed liberty of Sunday inspires panic (oxygen that becomes suffocating). Indeed at first, the *cachot* is the only place Caroline wants to be: its limits seem secure. But the text's allusion to Moreau shows that the *cachot* is externally imposed and stands for a unidimensional, dependent identity.

A more desirable form of identity (and one in tune with Glissant's *Tout-Monde*), on the other hand, is seen as various, multiform, entitled to *escape* from any attempt to define it from the outside, whether in 1797 or 2007. The tiny space of the Antilles may naturally invite introspection: but the islands have such peculiarly chaotic properties — their population is so resistant to Moreau's ordered explanations, for instance — that they quickly deflect the inward gaze, forcing it off outwards to connect with the rest of a world that itself 'nous déroute depuis les infinis de ses complexités' (24) (disorientates us from deep in its infinite, unfinished complexities) and is thus 'un prisme imprévisible qui diffracte les recoins de nos imaginaires' (24) (an unpredictable prism that diffracts the dark reaches of our imaginaries). Achieving such freedom depends on an attitude of mind and an act of subjective autonomy: it is necessary to '[f]asciner son cachot, défaire les murs, ouvrir le monde' (28) (master one's *cachot*, bring down the walls, open the world).

As a method for undermining the various forms of *cachot*, Chamoiseau points to the potential of literature. Within the first diegesis, for example, this notion is supported by the connexion between Caroline and the process of reading: to begin with, she 'regardait les pierres avec l'air de déchiffrer un texte' (39) (was looking at the stones as if deciphering a text); at the end she is persuaded to leave the *cachot* by Patrick's story. At a higher narratological level, Chamoiseau's shifting, diffracting narrator can be seen as an emblem of his call to wide-openness, while his restless, layered narration also disturbs the reader so as to 'défaire ses murs' (bring down her walls).

Variety, movement and uncertainty in the composition—or in the reading—of the narrative allow the subject to escape the confines of restrictive definitions imposed from elsewhere. This is confirmed in the novel's closing pages, where the narrator praises Faulkner, Saint-John Perse, Césaire and Glissant for the 'obscurity' of their writing that preserves freedom of meaning through 'l'incertain' (uncertainty), opposed to the imprisonment of 'transparence' (347), for '[c]'est en restant indécidable qu'une liberté peut ouvrir à toutes les libertés' (347) (it is by remaining undecidable that one form of freedom can open up into all kinds of freedom). Chamoiseau would no doubt gladly acknowledge the debt, contained in this vision, to Glissant's concept of 'opacité' (opacity), or the fundamental, secret unknowability of one individual by another, cultivated as a strategy for resisting domination.[11]

Chamoiseau's novel, then, appears to be a hopeful call—and not his first—for aesthetics as also a kind of politics. It fits seamlessly into a particular kind of postcolonial emphasis on the fluid subjectivity of subaltern identity groups, allied to their resistance to domination; and in Glissantian manner, it hints that political and cultural subordination can be transcended by a global, cosmopolitan openness, with art as the privileged vehicle of liberation.

However, this entire edifice, in Chamoiseau's text, is nevertheless built on an inescapable, near-polar relationship between the Antilles and metropolitan France: the text insists for example that Moreau, with his imprisoning desire for clarity, was of European origin (26), and educated in France; moreover the narrator emphasizes the strong hand of the contemporary metropole in defining the restrictive masks to be worn during the working week. On the other hand, the descriptions of rainy Sundays with the writer 'shattered by writing', together with the 'undecidable', 'globalizing', 'openness' of racial mixing that defeats Moreau, are identified as unmistakably Caribbean. Thus, the two principal terms of the book's title can be seen as an oxymoronic allusion to 'opaque' Antillean culture, associated with freedom and artistic creation (*Un Dimanche*) pitted against the metropole's urge to imprison by means of standardization and clarity (*au cachot*).

From Chamoiseau's perspective, on the evidence of this novel, the metropolitan–Antillean relationship is, then, still heavily structured by binary opposition, arguably more colonial than postcolonial, and characterized not only by complexities but incompatibilities. The dominant metaphor of imprisonment, and the artist's attempts to write his way out of it, clearly echo the tension I mentioned earlier, between the Antilles' political and economic incorporation into the Republic on the one hand, and their cultural distinctiveness and distance from the metropole on the other. Indeed, as much as political or cultural commentary, *Un Dimanche* might also be read as the troubled autofictional projection of an individual struggling with the accumulated bonds of his real-life work and art: after all, while Chamoiseau is a creative writer and pro-independence activist, as his own ironic references remind us he nevertheless works for the French *fonction publique* in an intrinsically conservative and culturally metropolitan institution. As Celia Britton points out in her discussion of Maud Mannoni, psychoanalysis can be critiqued as 'an agent of Western cultural imperialism and of colonial order':[12] the same could no doubt be said of social work. Chamoiseau's discussion of work and writing in *Un Dimanche* thus captures the paradoxes of the Antillean situation very acutely.

Pineau's *Folie, aller simple* is more identifiably autobiographical (although not diary-documentary) and set in metropolitan France, where Pineau works. Her text shows a number of similarities to Chamoiseau's. First, Gisèle too is aware of working within a rigid and somehow sacrosanct French *system*. She notes ironically that '[p]orter une blouse blanche dans une unité de soins psychiatriques, ce n'est pas seulement afficher une autorité ou un pouvoir, c'est (. . .) se poser en référent des lieux, gardien du temple, ange de la guérison, missionnaire en sacerdoce' (*F*, 64) (wearing a white uniform in a psychiatric care unit is not only displaying a kind of authority or power, it's (. . .) setting oneself up as a symbol for the whole place, a guardian of the temple, an angel of healing, a missionary with a priestly vocation). Like Patrick, she refers to the repertoire of role-play she uses to get the job done: 'hausser le ton comme au théâtre, froncer les sourcils et jouer à l'infirmière sévère pour rétablir la paix' (67) (raising your voice as you would in the theatre, frowning and playing the strict nurse to restore calm).

Second, Gisèle's identity is similarly supple, shifting and watchful to Patrick's: she explicitly declares herself both nurse *and* writer, Creole *and* French-speaking, distributed between the Caribbean *and* metropolitan France. As in *Un Dimanche*, this is echoed metaphorically in the text: throughout the hours recounted in the book, Gisèle involuntarily pictures the patient who has absconded earlier in the day to throw herself under a train. The images of a violently dismembered body that flash repeatedly into Gisèle's imagination replicate the inner fragmentation both of her damaged patients and of herself.

Yet Gisèle fully embraces her position as a professional carer, repeatedly referring to her responsibilities, the history and techniques of the role, and her identification with it when she is in a professional situation. Her play-acting — a voluntary tactic, adopted for the better performance of her job — arguably dramatizes in this instance a certain implication in the establishment more than estrangement from it.

In addition, Gisèle's expression of her own racial and cultural difference from most French citizens sits easily with her readiness to identify with the patients. She explicitly acknowledges that, like them, she inhabits a marginal border-zone: while she shares daily in their existence poised between lucidity and delusion, order and disorder, even life and death, she also shifts between her own disciplined, compassionate profession and her often violent, disturbing novels. She experiences the writing of these works as a 'delirium' that suggests an affinity with the patients. But a deeper, and even simpler, identification is suggested by Gisèle's view that writing has indeed saved her from actual clinical madness. There are cases of madness in her family, some of them directly related to the history of Guadeloupe: Gisèle's grandfather was traumatized by the First World War; other instances, including unstable periods of Gisèle's own youth, hint at a connexion to the collective intergenerational trauma of slavery. Looking at her patients, Gisèle remembers the words of Marie Didier: 'Tu aurais pu être pareil à ces fous; ils auraient pu être pareils à toi' (7) (you could have been the same as these mad people; they could have been the same as you). It is Gisèle's creative imagination and writing that have rescued her.

In a previous work, *Mes quatre femmes*, Pineau uses these lines as an epigraph:

> *La mémoire est une geôle.*
> *Là, les temps sont abolis.*
> *Là, les morts et les vivants sont ensemble.*
> *Là, les existences se réinventent à l'infini.*[13]
>
> (Memory is a jail.
> There, tenses are abolished.
> There, the dead and the living are together.
> There, existences are reinvented in infinite ways.)

The four women of the title — all members of Gisèle's family — speak throughout the text from a dark, jail-like space that recalls slavery, just as Chamoiseau's *cachot* does; but the four voices also move out beyond the *cachot* by dint of imagination just as Gisèle does in her writing, and just as Chamoiseau calls on us all to do in search of the 'diffracting prism' of the world. Pineau suggests more forcefully than Chamoiseau that history and memory can be damaging — that through fetishizing them one risks, in Fanon's famous phrase, becoming 'the slave of the Slavery that dehumanized [one's] ancestors'.[14] But she also sees memory releasing and sustaining creative imaginings, which can be conciliatory and even healing.

Where Chamoiseau's movement outwards and beyond confinement — his diffraction towards a further diffracting 'prism' — is associated with a sudden deflection and 'shattering' of perspective, therefore, Pineau's follows a smoother transition characterized by empathy and solidarity. One could cite in illustration of Gisèle's 'escape' from prisons such as history, introspection and the imposition of a social role, the examples of her solidarity with the psychiatric patients, and with the four women in the paradoxically elastic prison of memory, all of whom represent the way in which imagining, writing, even suffering delusions like the psychiatric patients, can be a way of overcoming pain as well as confinement. There is also, however, her pleasure in simple contact with the rest of society. Unlike Chamoiseau's narrator, for whom being French and Antillean seems a constant state of discomfort and incompatibility, Pineau's leaves the enclosed space of her shift at the end of the day only too happy to merge into the crowd of her compatriots: 'Plus que quelques mètres à parcourir et je pourrai dévaler les escaliers, m'engouffrer dans le métro, me mêler de nouveaux aux gens ordinaires' (231) (Just a few more metres to go and I'll be able to run down the stairs, be swallowed up by the metro, mingle once again with ordinary people). This unusually positive representation of being swallowed up by the métro strikingly underlines Gisèle's willing incorporation into the métro-pole, as well as her apparent confidence in her own individuality among the crowd, an individuality she owes partly to the cultural and racial ties to Guadeloupe she repeatedly recalls. Pineau's evocations of 'connectedness', then, are immediate, personal and involve a lived experience of proximity to other human beings, while Chamoiseau's are ambitiously global but theoretical, intellectual and abstract. The overriding impression created by Pineau is that differences can best be transcended by the human warmth of contact with 'ordinary people'. One final quotation from *Folie* is exemplary in this regard:

Autrefois, enfant, je ramassais des coquillages sur la plage pour en faire des tableaux. (. . .) La plupart étaient émoussées, ébréchés, brisés. (. . .) j'imaginais qu'ils avaient tous souffert de quelque chose, d'une mauvaise rencontre au fond des mers, d'une existence miséreuse. (. . .) Je leur inventais une histoire. (. . .) Tels les coquillages jonchant les plages de la Guadeloupe, les personnes qui se trouvent à l'hôpital psychiatrique arrivent d'un long voyage. (11–14)

(Long ago, as a child, I collected shells on the beach to make pictures. (. . .) Most of them were dulled, chipped, broken. (. . .) I imagined that they had all been through some sort of suffering, some terrible encounter at the bottom of the seas, some miserable existence. (. . .) I invented a story for them. (. . .) Like the shells strewn on the beaches of Guadeloupe, people who find themselves in psychiatric hospital have been on a long journey.)

In Gisèle's comparison between her Parisian patients and the shells washed up on a Guadeloupean beach she finds, rather than opposition, a poignant similarity that bridges gaps: geographical, racial, cultural, clinical, as well as the gap between Gisèle's job and her story-telling. It speaks of an empathy with the potential to transcend cultural or historical polarities, and of a readiness to embrace integration — albeit without homogenization. More importantly, by posing the explicitly Guadeloupean shells as the first term of her analogy, Gisèle discreetly 'centres' her comparison on the Antilles, casting her metropolitan patients as the secondary and peripheral element of the simile in a reversal of the usual centre–periphery relationship where the metropole generally figures as the 'central' norm and yardstick of any comparison. Thus Pineau hints that while Antilleans are damaged by history and must transcend the 'jail' of memory, *anyone* can be damaged by random misfortune (such as mental illness). Her response to metro-Antillean relations, far from resorting to binary oppositions, is to look for human reconciliation, partly through care as exemplified by nursing, partly via the creative imagination. Perhaps the pieces of France's cultural body can never (nor ever should) be fixed together in a single, static pattern; but empathy and imagination can somehow help Antilleans and metropolitans to a more effective mutual understanding that might one day mirror the constitutionally integrated France that encompasses them all.

The exploitation of labour was *the* essential feature of the slave economy whose traces still haunt Antillean writers (as these texts show). Yet early Antillean writings from the period that established slavery very rarely discuss slaves' work from their perspective.

Jean-Baptiste Du Tertre, one of the islands' earliest chroniclers, writing in 1667, is more compassionate than other early modern authors and, reporting the pitiful state of the slaves, deems their work in particular to be 'extrêmement fascheux' (extremely unpleasant), due to 'la chaleur du pays (...), l'humeur fascheuse des Commandeurs (...), [et] l'infructuosité de ce travail; car ils sçavent bien que toutes leurs sueurs vont au profit de leurs maistres'[15] (the heat of the country (...), the irritable humour of the Overseers (...) [and] the fruitlessness of their toil; for they know quite well that all their sweat is spent for the profit of their masters). Du Tertre is of his age in expressing the notion of labour as the origin of personal property and wealth. But he is almost unique in 150 years' pre-abolitionist writing about the Antilles in attributing to slaves the autonomous subjectivity to care about ownership of their work, or to have any possible vision of personal wealth.

Perhaps this early invisibility of work has left its mark today: while fictional characters are superficially identified with a wide range of jobs, there is almost no sustained focus on the established contemporary workplace in any recent Antillean literature, despite the fact that Antillean society displays many features of a work-orientated, capitalist economy (including high unemployment rates[16]). Chamoiseau's and Pineau's texts are welcome innovations, exploring difficult and paradoxical territory for the Antillean subject, for both narrators participate through work in national, metropolitan-based institutions constructed to restore order to unruly or marginal elements of society: in other words, each narrator — like each of the authors — is the agent of a dominant, integrative dynamic that operates both politically (re-affirming incorporation of the DROM into the metropole) and individually (bringing the disorderly adolescent or patient back into the fold of 'normal' society).

To borrow from recent scholarship by Christopher Miller and Bill Marshall,[17] one might say that these authors cannot help but 'write' themselves 'Atlantically', in that their texts are imbued with constant reference to both the Antilles and metropolitan France, as well as to the circulation of ideas and people around the Atlantic, from the slave trade to the present day. As members of a 'minority' culture located within the bounds of the French Republic itself, whose experience as citizens is never fully acknowledged in dominant, 'hexagonal' narratives of French identity, they can scarcely do otherwise: French Antillean identity cannot avoid being situated in a priority connexion to both the history of slavery and the metropole.

The same perspective cannot be applied conversely, however: most metropolitan French citizens perceive no need to situate themselves within a constant play of reference to the Antilles: the conscious appreciation of reciprocal cultural 'métissage' or 'mongrelization'[18] remains the preserve of a small minority, as Christopher Miller regrets,[19] and the Antillean experience still receives scant attention in the grand scheme of 'national' narratives.[20] If DROM writers, who are also French writers, wish to disrupt Eurocentric notions of Frenchness, they must find ways to stimulate 'Atlantic' thinking in their metropolitan compatriots by raising metropolitan consciousness about the *ultramarin* experience.

This is not the place for an investigation of the extent to which the writers under discussion attempt, or have any chance of success in, that specific enterprise. Although Chamoiseau and Pineau are published in Paris and Chamoiseau in particular is 'packaged' for as wide a market as possible,[21] it is necessary, as Huggan points out, to guard against the 'monumentalisation of a metropolitan readership, implied or not, for postcolonial texts'.[22] Jonathan Culler expresses a similar view in his enthusiastic discussion of Anderson's concept of 'imagined communities', noting further that Anderson's most powerful claim about the novel is not, as some critics have assumed, about 'the way some novels, by their contents, help to encourage, shape, justify or legitimate the nation' (or indeed a particular version of it), but, in general terms, to 'make the form of the novel a condition of imagining the nation: a structural condition of possibility' based on a new way of conceiving of time and space.[23] Nevertheless, by their constant reference to the metro-Antillean axis, and not least by 'staging' themselves as marginal in relation to dominant French metropolitan culture, while yet contributing to certain of that very culture's key institutions by their own professional employment, both Chamoiseau and Pineau raise questions about the 'imagined community' that is the French nation, to the point where '[o]ne might say (. . .) that the[ir] posited audience is those who could recognize that the community being described is, if not a nation, one about which it is an issue whether it is a nation'.[24]

This has implications for how we frame our reading of the Antilles as researchers. With the impetus towards 'Transnational French Studies'[25] and 'Atlantic Studies', scholars have been encouraged to relax their focus on the nation state,[26] and specifically on the Hexagon, in order to attend to the interactions, in Marshall's phrase, of a 'de-centred, non-hierarchical reconceptualization of France and its constituent and connected spaces and territories, and of French cultures in general'.[27] In this movement we find, once again, a general (and entirely welcome) emphasis on exchange and openness, as well as an egalitarian corrective to outmoded academic perspectives. What 'transnational' readings of the Antilles will avoid, however, is the unnuanced projection of this *analytical* agenda into our understanding of the Antilles themselves, for it is precisely the islands' continued belonging to a Eurocentric nation state that makes their situation so acutely complex. The 'Frenchness' of Antilleans is continually highly visible to them via material objects and experiences such as identity cards, education, policing, banks and shops; indeed, the largest source of power and money available to promote Antillean culture itself lies ultimately with the national Ministry in Paris. Thus, however much postcolonial writers and theorists, including Caribbean ones, promote structures of thought that circulate restlessly beyond hierarchical dualities, the DROM keep in simultaneous play a more linear, binary configuration that crackles with the energy of intra-Republican tensions.

When we reconsider our two texts through these overlaid frameworks — the multidirectional and chaotic, complemented by the polar and linear — the authors' invitation to their audience comes into sharper focus, showing how these texts embody the tension of difference and integration I described at the start of this essay. Chamoiseau's opaque, 'diffracting' narrative attempts to 'bring down the walls' of his readers by a direct, confrontational challenge, refusing transparency, insisting on Antillean difference, and seeking continually to escape the binary colonial anxieties of the Antillean situation... which it thereby paradoxically — and heavily — underlines. Pineau presents a less theorized, more experiential but confidently integrative 'transcultural' vision, in which her exemplary, de-centring image of beached shells represents an 'Atlantic' tactic. By centring her comparison of patients and shells on Guadeloupe, Pineau invites readers less to 'bring down their walls' than to loosen the imprisoning imaginary boundaries that identify the metropole with the nation, and to stretch the frontiers of the French 'imagined community' until its contours coincide with the political reality of a Republic that includes small Caribbean islands. Unless or until the latter leave the Republic (currently an unlikely scenario, in part because of benefits like French welfare and health care, as described by our two authors), this very reality of their Frenchness will remain a key factor in the analysis of Antillean literature, as both Chamoiseau and Pineau demonstrate.

NOTES

I am grateful to the British Academy for the grant that enabled the research for this article, and to the editors of this volume and to Margaret-Anne Hutton for helpful advice.

1 Celia Britton, *Edouard Glissant and Postcolonial Theory: Strategies of Language and Resistance* (Charlottesville and London: University of Virginia Press, 1999).

2 Edouard Glissant, *Poetics of Relation*, translated by Betsy Wing (Ann Arbor: University of Michigan Press, 1997); *Le Traité du Tout-Monde* (Paris: Gallimard, 1997).

3 While the near-unanimous convention is for scholars to adopt broadly postcolonial approaches to Antillean culture, those who most carefully acknowledge the islands' particular situation as DROM include (amongst others) Britton, *Edouard Glissant and Postcolonial Theory*; J. Michael Dash, 'Postcolonial Thought and the Francophone Caribbean' in *Francophone Postcolonial Studies, a Critical Introduction*, edited by Charles Forsdick and David Murphy (London: Arnold, 2003), 231–41; Maeve McCusker, *Patrick Chamoiseau: Recovering Memory* (Liverpool: Liverpool University Press, 2007); H. Adlai Murdoch, 'Autobiography and Departmentalization in Chamoiseau's *Chemin d'école*: Representational Strategies and the Martinican Memoir', *Research in African Literatures* 40:2 (2009), 16–39. For an analysis strongly influenced by Glissant, see Elizabeth Bowles Duchanaud, *Reading the French Caribbean through Edouard Glissant: New Approaches to Condé, Chamoiseau, Schwarz-Bart, and Chauvet* (Saarbrücken: VDM Verlag, 2009); for a brilliant discussion of the 'hyperrelational culture of the Caribbean' that draws on Glissant amongst others, see Mary Gallagher, *Soundings in French Caribbean Writing since 1950: The Shock of Space and Time* (Oxford: Oxford University Press, 2002).

4 Not that the study of any 'postcolony' can ever be simple or generic. For an insightful discussion of postcolonial studies' inherent eclecticism and discontinuities, see Nicholas Harrison, *Postcolonial Criticism. History, Theory and the Work of Fiction* (Cambridge: Polity, 2003).

5 Benedict Anderson, *Imagined Communities: Reflections on the Origin and Spread of Nationalism* (London and New York: Verso, revised edition 1991).

6 Patrick Chamoiseau, *Un dimanche au cachot* (Paris: Gallimard 'Folio', 2007), henceforward referred to as *DC*; Gisèle Pineau, *Folie, aller simple. Journée ordinaire d'une infirmière* (Paris: Philippe Rey, 2010), henceforward referred to as *F*.

7 I use first names to refer to the characters and surnames for the authors.

8 Graham Huggan uses this term for the 'process by which marginalised groups or individuals are moved to dramatise their "subordinate" status for

the benefit of a majority or mainstream audience', often with 'a critical or even subversive function'. See Huggan, *The Postcolonial Exotic: Marketing the Margins* (London and New York: Routledge, 2001), 87.

9 See Lorna Milne, 'Patrick Chamoiseau, mise en abyme et "diffraction"' in *Tracées de Patrick Chamoiseau*, edited by Samia Kassab-Charfi, special issue of *Interculturel Francophonies* (November–December 2012), 129–41.

10 M. L. E. Moreau de Saint-Méry, *Description topographique, physique, civile, politique et historique de la partie française de l'isle Saint-Domingue*, 3 vols. (Philadelphia: chez l'auteur, au coin de Front et de Callow-Hill streets, 1797).

11 'Opacité' is one of the key concepts explored by Britton in *Edouard Glissant and Postcolonial Theory*.

12 Celia Britton, *Race and the Unconscious: Freudianism in French Caribbean Thought* (Oxford: Legenda, 2002), 51.

13 Gisèle Pineau, *Mes quatre femmes* (Paris: Philippe Rey, 2005).

14 Frantz Fanon, *Black Skin, White Masks*, translated by Charles Lam Markmann (London: Pluto Press, 2008), 179.

15 Jean-Baptiste Du Tertre, *Histoire Générale des Antilles habitées par les François*, 2nd edition, Vol. 2 (Paris: Thomas Jolly, 1667–71), 525.

16 See http://www.insee.fr/fr/themes/detail.asp?reg_id=99&ref_id=chomage-zone-2010, consulted 22 July 2013, 8.00pm.

17 Christopher Miller, *The French Atlantic Triangle. Literature and Culture of the Slave Trade* (Durham, NC: Duke University Press, 2008); Bill Marshall, *The French Atlantic. Travels in Culture and History* (Liverpool: Liverpool University Press, 2009).

18 Françoise Lionnet, '"Logiques métisses": Cultural Appropriation and Postcolonial Representations', *College Literature* 19/20:3/1 (Oct. 1992–Feb. 1993), 100–20.

19 Miller, *The French Atlantic Triangle*, 385–90.

20 A simple example can be seen in Philippe Poirrier and René Rizzardo, *Une Ambition partagée? La coopération entre le ministère de la Culture et les collectivités territoriales (1959–2009)* (Paris: Comité d'histoire du ministère de la culture, 2009). This volume celebrates fifty years of the Ministry for Culture and the supposed 'decentralization' of French cultural administration with contributions from around the various regions. As I have pointed out elsewhere, it contains not one piece about any of the DROM. See L. Milne, review of the above volume in *H-France*, 10:202 (December 2010), www.h-france.net/vol10reviews/vol10no202milne.pdf, consulted 22 July 2013, 8.30pm.

21 See Richard Watts, *Packaging Post/coloniality. The Manufacture of Literary Identity in the Francophone World* (Lanham, MD: Lexington, 2004).

22 Huggan, *The Postcolonial Exotic*, 30.

23   'When we are discussing the audience for novels, we need to avoid unwarranted presumptions about both the novels' address — the readerly role they construct — and their actual audiences.' Jonathan Culler, *The Literary in Theory* (Stanford: Stanford University Press, 2007), 70.

24   Culler, *The Literary in Theory*, 60. Culler is discussing Anderson's analysis of Rizal and Balzac.

25   Alec G. Hargreaves, Charles Forsdick and David Murphy, *Transnational French Studies: Postcolonialism and Littérature-Monde* (Liverpool: Liverpool University Studies, 2012).

26   This perspective would appeal to Chamoiseau, as demonstrated most explicitly in the suggestively named *Quand les murs tombent. L'identité nationale hors-la-loi? (When the Walls Come Down. National Identity Outlawed?)*, co-authored with Edouard Glissant (Paris: Galaade, 2007).

27   Marshall, *The French Atlantic,* 12.

Just a Case of Mistaken Ancestors? Dramatizing Modernisms in Maryse Condé's *Heremakhonon*

Eva Sansavior

Abstract:

The marked intertextual patterning of Maryse Condé's first novel *Heremakhonon* is a widely acknowledged feature, with the relationship between Condé's novel and Aimé Césaire's *Notebook of a Return to my Native Land* attracting the bulk of critical attention. Through close readings of to date unexamined dramatic codes in *Heremakhonon*, this article proposes to extend the cultural context in which Condé's text is traditionally read. Moving beyond the standard critical discussions of authenticity, I track *Heremakhonon*'s mobile positionings in relation to polarizing debates in the broader French literary-critical field between *engagement* and modernism. This focus allows for an exploration of the complex sets of relationships between the cultures of modernism and *engagement* that provide the conditions of possibility for Condé's novel.

Keywords: Maryse Condé, Aimé Césaire, Frantz Fanon, Jean-Paul Sartre authenticity, modernism, political engagement

In this article I argue for bringing an attention to the dramatic codes that structure Maryse Condé's first novel, *Heremakhonon*. My discussion will explore the various ways in which these codes put into play and mine the dramatic potential of one of the defining debates in the French literary-critical field after the Second World War between, on the one hand, Sartrean *engagement* and, on the other, modernist formalism. This debate came to public prominence from the 1960s onwards thanks to its main exponent Jean-Paul Sartre, and key thinkers associated with the *nouveau roman* such as Alain Robbe-Grillet. At stake is the question of what constitutes the proper or 'authentic'

Paragraph 37.2 (2014): 221–234
DOI: 10.3366/para.2014.0123
© Edinburgh University Press
www.euppublishing.com/para

role of literature in its relation to the individual and society. As I shall illustrate, this exploratory, constantly shifting process relies for its dramatic potency on the particularizing and restless staging of what may be called the *Zeitgeist* of this period, in a distinctively individual space: the framing consciousness of the novel's protagonist, Véronica Mercier. In the fragmented reflections of this Guadeloupean intellectual from a prosperous middle-class background who leaves France to work as a teacher in an African country reminiscent of 1960s Guinea, the seemingly abstract philosophical questions of the day are transmuted as topical questions bristling with an urgency that is as much individual as collective (although, and perhaps precisely *because* this latter dimension is disavowed with such stridency by Véronica).

Condé's first-hand experiences of the complexities of moral and political expediencies in the newly independent African nations had undoubtedly provided her with formative experiential coordinates for mapping provisional responses to the questions highlighted above. Published in 1976 under the title 'Heremakhonon' Condé's commercially unsuccessful first novel was re-issued in 1988 under the title 'En attendant le bonheur'.[1] However, by the time the text had established Condé as a novelist, she was already a well-known dramatist, whose plays mined the rich terrain of her experiences in Africa in the 1950s and 1960s (a career which she continues in parallel today with her literary and critical writing).[2]

From the outset, *Heremakhonon*'s protagonist Véronica characterizes the motivations for her journey in terms of a search for her lost African origins and, in the course of the novel, she attempts to realize this aim through what turns out to be an unsuccessful relationship with the corrupt government minister, Saliou. By the end of the novel, following the disappearance of one of her politically active students and the country's inexorable slide into bloody civil unrest, Véronica has abandoned her quest and is on her way back to France having recognized that she has simply got 'the wrong ancestors'. The elements of the text's narrative that I have highlighted here and Véronica's bald assertion at the end of the novel, 'I got the wrong ancestors',[3] have led to comparisons with Aimé Césaire's *Notebook of a Return to My Native Land*. However, the acknowledgment of these affinities has typically served as a pretext for downplaying — if not dismissing altogether — the need to examine the productively ambivalent relationship that Condé's novel in fact establishes with Césaire's seminal work.[4] Moreover, it is the thematic affinities between the texts that have been the object of exclusive critical attention. In line with this, comparative readings of the identity quest in both texts have served the established critical assumption that Condé's novel can quite simply be viewed as *transcending* Césaire's inauthentic identitarian position.[5]

My argument in this paper situates itself in contrast to such readings of Condé's text. My aim here is to take the assumed authenticity/inauthenticity dichotomy that is mobilized in comparative discussions of Condé's and Césaire's texts as an invitation to move beyond seemingly irreconcilable positions. My analysis will mirror the strategies of Condé's text, and perform successive 'soundings' of the very terms of authenticity and inauthenticity so as to release a mobile and necessarily culturally diverse range of dramatic potentialities. At the centre of this undertaking will be a concern with reading the novel outside of its taken-for-granted Afro-centric cultural boundaries with a view to mapping the complex range of intertextual dialogues that it establishes within and between the different Francophone Caribbean, French and African-American texts that it references.

The preoccupation that launches the novel, Véronica's exasperated insistence on the originality of her planned trip to Africa, immediately foregrounds her ambivalence to a primary literary model for her quest: Césaire's *Notebook of a Return to My Native Land*. Given the centrality of the intertextual relationship that the novel establishes with Césaire's text, Véronica's insistence on the originality of her quest is perhaps necessarily unreliable. There are in fact marked similarities between the context of the production of Césaire's text and the intellectual and cultural milieu that Véronica describes at the start of *Heremakhonon*. Written in 1939, *Notebook of a Return to My Native Land* is widely considered to be the founding text of the *Négritude* movement, a movement dedicated to the definition of a distinctive black identity. A significant body of recent scholarship has situated the *Négritude* project within a more extensive history of black consciousness movements that brought together African-American, African and Caribbean intellectuals from the beginning of the twentieth century in Paris.[6] One study, in particular, Michel Fabre's *From Harlem to Paris: Black American Writers in France 1840–1980* stresses that the evolution of these movements is best understood not as a linear process with the ideas of one group feeding directly into another but, rather, as a more oblique, multi-directional process.[7] Fabre illustrates that this multi-directionality is a defining feature of the historical development of all these movements, one that is articulated throughout the whole period of their development. These multi-directional influences were generative in both institutional and textual terms. They are at work in the major black consciousness movements that emerge in the 1930s and 1940s such as The New Negro and Harlem Renaissance movements. Similarly, multi-directional influences can be tracked across individual literary works such as René Maran's anti-colonialist novel *Batouala* (winner of the Prix Goncourt in 1921) and Claude McKay's 1929 novel *Banjo*. At a broad level, therefore, these various studies of transatlantic black cultures suggest that Francophone and African-American black consciousness movements and their textual manifestations can be situated within a transatlantic black modernist culture that expressed a common preoccupation with defining an aesthetic appropriate to the representation of an authentic black identity. I propose to extend the multi-directionality that is an increasingly accepted feature of the development of transatlantic modernisms to my discussion of the relationships that are constructed between transatlantic and Euro-American modernisms in *Heremakhonon*. Black cultures of modernism — of which Césaire's *Notebook of a Return to My Native Land* served as a foundational text — simultaneously drew on and contributed towards a broader international modernist cultural and aesthetic experience.[8] Recent studies of modernism cited above have done much to challenge its taken-for-granted (Euro-centric) universalism by accounting for the specific preoccupations of various cultures of modernism. However, this focus has also been to the detriment of substantive critical engagement with the shared influences of apparently divergent cultures of modernism. In the introduction to the Bloodaxe bilingual edition of Césaire's *Notebook of a Return to My Native Land*, Mireille Rosello situates the genesis of Césaire's text and the *Négritude* project within the 'negrophilia' that had shaped European tastes from the early twentieth century. Crucially, as Rosello highlights, this was a trend that permeated a broad range of artistic disciplines from the visual arts to music and dance.[9] Thus, Rosello's analysis brings to the fore the key role of the performing arts in providing what can be characterized as a 'nexus of dissemination' for the shared negrophilic cultural models on which transatlantic and Euro-American modernist works would build.

Heremakhonon undoubtedly derives its dramatic material and intensity from the unsettling of the precepts that govern these two broad cultures of modernism along with the assumed fixity of the boundaries between these cultures. Both strategies are in evidence in the novel's opening paragraph:

Honestly! You'd think I'm going because it is the in thing to do. Africa is very much the thing to do lately. Europeans and a good many others are writing volumes on it. Arts and craft centres are opening up all over the Left Bank. Blondes are dyeing their lips with henna and running to the open market for their peppers (...). Well, I'm not! (*H*, 3)

Véronica's double bind, tersely acknowledged and disavowed above, provides the structuring conflict for the unfurling 'drama of consciousness' tracked across this novel. Her appeal to an individually directed original identity quest centred on Africa, is arguably shaped by a paradoxical modernist 'anxiety of influence' that would disavow all precursors (whether modernist or Césairian). Nevertheless, this initial framing of her quest relies on the conflation of two apparently irreconcilable positions: on the one hand, the famous modernist injunction to 'make new' and, on the other, the Césairian belief in the possibility of reclaiming an authentic 'engaged' African identity. The 'seriousness' of this drama is, however, always threatened by Véronica's 'post-modern' awareness of the inherent performativity of all positions.[10] Véronica's ironic musings suggest that a passion for all things African is creating a type of federative trans–cultural social space that would allow this passion to be expressed in a variety of ways. Furthermore, a compulsion to perform 'Africanness' is crossing the cultural divide between high and low culture, with the city providing various theatrical sites (shops, the market and the street) and the related props to facilitate various individual (and to some extent improvisatory) performances. Véronica's choice of words in this opening paragraph therefore underscores the central — if paradoxical — role of African culture as a shared marker for authenticity in black and European modernisms and, in particular, its role in generating various dramatic performances.

It is clear, however, that Véronica's status as a sophisticated intellectual is inextricable from her avowed scepticism towards such naïve performances. The sceptical stance that she adopts in relation to these representations is mirrored by her parents' imagined dismissive attitude towards her trip to Africa conveyed in their facial gestures: 'I can see them now. My mother, sighing as usual and my father pinching his thin lips' (*H*, 3). Véronica's journey at this stage is motivated by a desire to move beyond the well-worn performances of a type of commodified African identity available within the metropolitan popular and intellectual cultural market places. Yet, it is her obsessively re-imagined familial context that simultaneously generates this desire for authenticity and circumscribes the possibilities for realizing this state.

Heremakhonon's attention to the depiction of Véronica's drama of consciousness provides a meta-dramatic frame in which to explore the text's ironic mimicry of modernist formal methods along with the implicit claim to authenticity that underpins these. In key respects, the novel's approach to characterization and narrative is indebted to European modernist aesthetic precepts. Véronica, the protagonist, never speaks directly and is assigned neither clear physical traits nor an objective personal story that would allow her to be identified as 'realistic'. In addition, there is no omniscient narrator to guarantee the authenticity of either the protagonist or her story. The narrative perspective is in fact entirely subjective. What the novel presents is not a 'story', in the traditional sense, but Véronica's fragmented interior monologue, a monologue threaded through with flashbacks, imaginary, dream-like scenes and filtered dialogue. However, the novel's apparent imitation of key elements of modernist literary aesthetics is turned towards a series of obsessive reflections on such 'outmoded' concepts as cultural authenticity and political engagement (even if these are disavowed).[11]

What activates Véronica's quest is precisely her anxiety-ridden perception of a gap in her 'story', the result of her father's failure to provide her with any information that would allow her to situate his triumphant representations of her family's social ascension in a broader history. The girl who questions her father about her African past is concerned to know about the time '[b]efore the family saga. The great-grandfather or the great-great-grandfather who had bought his freedom with a lot of patience and hard work' (*H*, 11). The familial universe is structured by two competing narratives: Césaire's *Notebook of a Return to My Native Land* and the aspirational African-American autobiographical narrative by Booker T. Washington, *Up from Slavery*:

Eia for the royal cailcedra. . .

His freedom is a plot of land. Set up house with Florimonde, an honest and hardworking negress Florimonde whose children had, one by one, climbed the rungs of the social ladder. Good old Booker T. (*H*, 11, translation adapted)

In this scene, Véronica's internal retelling of the heroic story of her ancestors' social mobility is framed by seemingly ventriloquized references to Césaire's *Notebook of a Return to My Native Land* and Booker T. Washington's *Up from Slavery*. On one level, this scene has the somewhat crazed energy of dramatic sequences structured around outbursts of non sequiturs associated with the Absurdist theatre of Eugène Ionesco and Samuel Beckett. However, the distinct material presence ascribed to the African-American and Francophone Caribbean texts in the narrative points to the contrasting possibilities that Véronica envisages for them in her drama of consciousness.

These differences become apparent in two theatrical frames: first, in the interplay between idiosyncratic references to African-American and Francophone Caribbean texts and Véronica's dramatized memories of her family's mimicry. Second, these differences are evident in Véronica's own (purely imaginary) stagings of elements of these same works. Two scenes, in particular, establish mimicry as the dominant dramatic model for Véronica's inauthentic familial context. In the first chapter of the novel, merely a few pages before her satirical recounting of her father's version of their ancestors' rise from slavery that I cited above, Véronica reproduces the memory of her father's contemptuous comments concerning the relationship between slavery and dancing. In this scene, the narrative appears to exploit creatively the dramatic potential of Léon-Gontran Damas's excoriating poetic reflections on the 'ridiculous' nature of inauthenticity in his poem 'Sale'.[12] From the first stanza of 'Sale' the poetic voice adopts a confessional tone that explodes in the final stanza into a violent repudiation of the colonial system:

> I feel ridiculous
> In their shoes
> In their tuxedo
> In their collar
> In their monocle
> In their bowler hat
>
> (...)
> I feel ridiculous
> Amongst them as an accomplice
> Amongst them as a supporter
> Amongst them as a murderer
> My hands horrifyingly red
> With the blood of their civ-il-iz-ation.
> (Léon-Gontran Damas, 'Sale', my translation)

In common with Damas's poetic voice above, Véronica recalls her father's comments with an attention to elements of dress, corporeal movements and voice that also serves to mark the memory as a performance of 'ridiculous' mimicry:

The Mandingo marabout used to say such dances should be forbidden. 'If they did not dance, they would already be free (...)'. *He*, of course was free. Free to no longer walk on the soles of his feet. Free to stick his neck in a bowtie and to welcome Sundays' guests with a pompous, 'Eloise, you look divine!' (*H*, 7)

However, Véronica's dramatization of her family's social pretensions has none of Damas's guilt-ridden acknowledgement of his own complicity with the inauthentic colonial system (nor, for that matter, the barely contained anti-colonial rage that erupts in the poem). In fact, underlying Véronica's mockery of her parents is what appears to be the self-satisfied belief that she is entirely immune to such social pretensions. In contrast with Damas's poetic alter ego, Véronica's dramatization of her parents' pretensions therefore emerges not as an act of contestation but as an end in itself.

If in the second scene, Véronica's attention turns explicitly towards the question of 'politics', it is once again her inauthentic familial context that is the backdrop for her reflections. African–American texts belonging to intellectual (Booker T. Washington) and popular cultures (*Ebony*) provide the 'script' for Véronica's imaginary dramatization of how she would be greeted on her return by her family:

If I went back, they would all be at the airport. The Mandingo marabout like the others. Dirty linen is kept in the family. And, in a way, I'm paying homage through the family to the whole race as I am studying at university in France. Booker T. Washington would not have hesitated to kiss me on both cheeks. And I would have my place in *Ebony*. (*H*, 14)

Véronica's reference to 'la Race' suggests that her sense of blackness is an international or transatlantic one. In contrast with the memory discussed above, which draws obliquely on Damas's poem (without explicitly naming the work), the ironic tone of her explicit references to these African–American works and cultural references suggest that they are merely names which, at best, provide free-floating, empty concepts co-opted for use within the familial culture of which she is a part. Véronica's distanced relationship to these narratives is doubled by their implicit presentation as de-politicized speech performances that serve merely to mask her parents' virulent class-based prejudices. Furthermore, Véronica's dismissive presentation of these performances arguably signals the limited viability of these African–American works for her individual drama.

In contrast, Véronica's engagement with the works of Fanon and Césaire points to the intensity of her intellectual and emotional implication in these works, an implication that is generative of a number of critically charged and open-ended 'performances'. In the following imaginary conversation between two fictional characters, Césaire's Christophe and Condé's Véronica, a quoted line from Césaire's play *The Tragedy of King Christophe* is framed by Véronica's sardonic inner dialogue, in which she questions the opinions expressed by the play's eponymous protagonist:

I don't agree with Césaire when he proclaims by the grace of Christophe: 'I ask too much of men. But not enough of black men, Madame.' I have read Césaire too like everybody else. I mean like everybody from our world, the Third World. In my opinion, it's high time they left the niggers in peace, let them dance, get drunk and make love. They've deserved it. (*H*, 71)

The ironic tone of this encounter underscores the ambivalent relationship that Véronica's drama of consciousness maintains with the broader dramatic tradition constituted by Césaire's oeuvre (one that both includes and extends beyond *Notebook of a Return to My Native Land*). As her imaginary exchange with Césaire's Christophe highlights, she is keen to assert her critical independence from Césaire's views (and implicitly the independence of her own internal drama). However, the central position assigned to the quotation from Césaire's play in this sequence may certainly be viewed as Véronica's tacit admission of a posture of essential *dependence*. This dramatic sequence therefore emerges as a type of critical supplement to Césaire's play and larger body of work.

Véronica's ambivalent scepticism towards the Césairian oeuvre in turn provides the rationale for her numerous references to Fanon's *Black Skin, White Masks* and *The Wretched of the Earth*. Through these references, Véronica's internal drama calls into question the implicit position of Césaire's *Notebook of a Return to My Native Land* as the dominant model for (her) 'black identity'. This is not to say, however, that Fanon's texts escape Véronica's critical dramatizations. While invoked as a challenge to Césaire's positions, Fanon's *Black Skin, White Masks* is nevertheless mined for its dramatic potential. Fanon's representation of the black female's predisposition towards lactification provides the context for a staging of Véronica's half-hearted self-defence against this charge. In the following quotation, the notion of lactification is used as a prompt for a mini court-room style drama in which Véronica alternates between two opposing positions: on the one hand, the side of the accusers whose position is presented in normal typeface and, on the other, the accused who articulates her defence in italics:

Once again, I loved those two men because I was in love. All those young black males my family introduced to me made me shudder. Why? *Not because they were black. Ridiculous! I'm no Mayotte Capécia. No! I'm not interested in whitening the race! I swear...* (H, 28)

Yet, the seriousness of this self-defence is undermined by Véronica's nostalgic musings very early in the novel on her adolescent infatuation with a mulatto boy:

This light-skinned mulatto with green eyes and the complexion of a young Oriental prince (a fifteen year old's comparisons are always silly). Since then I have never gotten over my fascination for light-colored eyes. Perhaps I already had it. Very likely. (H, 6)

A key feature of these reflections is Véronica's ambivalent complication of the clear-cut positions of authenticity and inauthenticity mobilized around the idea of lactification in Fanon's *Black Skin, White Masks*.[13] On one level, in characterizing this attraction as an illness from which she is 'never cured', Véronica appears to admit her own 'inauthentic' susceptibility towards the 'self-whitening' that Fanon denounces. But the self-criticism implicit in this remembrance is undercut by an ironic puzzling over the 'origins' of this fascination. The unresolved quality of this puzzling would suggest that Véronica chooses not, as Fanon might envisage, to reject her inauthenticity, but rather to assume a posture of ceaseless and dramatically charged questioning *in relation* to it.

A similar commitment to open-ended dramatizations of her own inauthenticity is paradoxically at work in Véronica's apparent dismissal of the second text by Fanon that she names: *The Wretched of the Earth.* Her admission that she has not read Fanon's seminal defence of anti-colonial violence, is not intended as a signal that she considers this work to be 'unproductive' for her internal drama. In spite of Véronica's apparent absence of engagement with Fanon's physical text, it is clear that the text's reputation (operating apparently independently from the material text) has the capacity to draw powerful dramatic responses from her. Some of these responses are in keeping with the dramatic range that she has displayed thus far. Early in the novel, for example, Véronica balks inwardly at her students' angry reflections on the social injustices perpetuated by the leaders of their newly independent nation:

They count your Mercedes and vent their anger against your wives' jewels. They say an oligarchy of greed has taken over from Europe. Instead of the Koran, they recite Fanon. Yesterday, they wanted to drag me into a discussion of *The Wretched of the Earth* that I have not read. Mea culpa! Mea maxima culpa! (*H*, 30)

Her admission that she has not read Fanon's *The Wretched of the Earth* is punctuated by the mixture of over-dramatic irony and self-defensiveness that has been defining features of her internal engagements with all the texts that she cites. But Véronica's musings at the end of the novel on her missed opportunity to join the people in an uprising suggest that Fanon's unread text perhaps has the power to inspire in her a certain nostalgic, albeit ephemeral, longing for authentic political engagement:

I imagine that if, that night, the city had not slept, if the men, women and youngsters had come out of their huts, then I would certainly have marched with them. Their determination would have given me strength. (*H*, 166, translation adapted)

The instability of this longing is underlined by the use of the verbal structure 'I imagine'; it would seem that Véronica is unconvinced by her own assertion of political will. Arguably, the romantic tone of this performance of belated political engagement effects a diversion of the revolutionary energies of Fanon's text; it is as though she is projecting herself into the role of a politically committed, heroic 'woman of the people' not as a dramatic precursor to *actual* engagement but purely for her own enjoyment (and, perhaps, also that of the reader). While Véronica conveys an infectious enthusiasm for this heroic identity, her self-conscious staging of this identity works to cast doubt on her expressed commitment to collective political action. This sense of doubt is intensified by the use of the conditional tense which effectively projects the performance itself and the real political engagement that it represents onto an imaginary plane. Crucially, it is also the possibility for Véronica's assumption of a 'politically engaged' collective identity that is projected onto this imaginary plane.

Indeed, Véronica's reflections that follow on from this scene at the end of the novel suggest that it is precisely such inauthentic performances that are intrinsic to her ambivalent claim to what is perhaps necessarily an indefinitely deferred identity. The tragic resonance brought to the possibility for political engagement itself is highlighted by dramatic borrowings from Sartre's tragedy about failed engagement, *Dirty Hands*. At the level of linguistic content, there are marked similarities between Véronica's final rueful reflections on the outcome of her identity quest and Hugo's comments to Olga at the end of *Dirty Hands* (just before he chooses suicide):

My ancestors led me on. What can I say? I looked for myself in the wrong place. In the arms of an assassin. Come now, don't use big words. Always dramatizing. (*H*, 167)

HUGO: No big words, Olga. There are too many big words in this story already and they have done much harm (*Dirty Hands*, Act VII).[14]

Yet this linguistic resonance between Condé's and Sartre's works serves as an evocative marker of the divergence between the two protagonists' positions. While Hugo's individual political engagement is 'recuperated' through his final rejection of 'big words' and his tragic act, it is ultimately to the dramatic potency of words that Véronica maintains a seemingly irresolvable emotional attachment.

In ending on this ironic dramatization of the impossibility of engagement, *Heremakhonon* manifests its formative divisions within the terms of the debate that I outlined in the introduction. On one level, this is a novel whose dramatic energies are undoubtedly nourished by a modernist suspicion of political engagement. At the same time, the closing reference to Sartre's *Dirty Hands* would suggest that a nostalgic attachment to an idea of political engagement also feeds Véronica's ceaselessly re-activated 'taste for drama'. It is this unresolved implication in questions of literary and political engagement that dictates the terms of Véronica's 'tragic drama' at the novel's close. In the final analysis, Véronica situates her failed quest in relation to two models of drama. The first model is that of tragedy in terms of which her failure might be read as 'pre-destined'. It is Véronica's familial drama that provides the terms of the second model, a model structured by what has been shown to be an impossible disavowal of role-play or mimicry (a disavowal that, paradoxically, identifies her as belonging to the very familial context from which she has sought to distance herself). The novel's ending thus problematizes the claims to authenticity that, arguably, underwrite all the various discursive positions that it dramatizes (whether modernist, Sartrean, African-American or Francophone Caribbean). What this novel ultimately effects is a revalorization of the uses of inauthenticity, figured variously as literary or dramatic traditions, familial or cultural legacies and, specifically, the dramatic potential of an enduring affective and intellectual attachment to various types of inauthentic precursors.

NOTES

1   The word 'Heremakhonon' is a Malinke word that translates in French as 'attend le bonheur' (waiting for happiness).

2   For a discussion of the evolution of Condé's theatre see Stéphanie Bérard, *Théâtres des Antilles, Traditions et scènes contemporaines* (préface d'Ina Césaire) (Paris: L'Harmattan, 2009).

3   Maryse Condé, *Heremakhonon: A Novel*, translated by Richard Philcox (Boulder, CO: Lynne Rienner, 2000), 3. All quotations are taken from this English translation of *En attendant le bonheur*, and will henceforth appear in the main text abbreviated to *H*.

4   Parts of this article have previously appeared in Eva Sansavior, *Maryse Condé and the Space of Literature* (Oxford: Legenda, 2012), 37–51.

5   For similar arguments see for example, Françoise Lionnet, *Autobiographical Voices: Race, Gender and Self-Portraiture* (Ithaca and London: Cornell University Press, 1989); Arlette M. Smith, 'The Semiotics of Exile: Maryse Condé's Fictional Works', *Callaloo*, 14 (1991), 381–88 (382); Christopher L. Miller, 'After Negation: Africa in Two Novels by Maryse Condé' in *Postcolonial Subjects: Francophone Women Writers*, edited by Mary Green et al. (Minneapolis and London: University of Minnesota Press, 1996), 173–85 (174).

6   See Paul Gilroy, *The Black Atlantic: Identity and Double Consciousness* (London: Verso, 1993); Maryse Condé, 'O Brave New World', *Research in African Literatures* 29 (1998), 1–7; Brent Hayes Edwards, *The Practice of Diaspora: Literature, Translation and the Rise of Black Internationalism* (Cambridge, MA and London: Harvard University Press, 2003); *Afro-Modern: Journey Through the Black Atlantic*, edited by Tanya Barson and Peter Gorschulter (London: Tate Publishing, 2008).

7   Michel Fabre, *From Harlem to Paris: Black American Writers in France 1840–1980* (Urbana and Chicago: University of Illinois Press, 1991), 4–8.

8   For a discussion of the contribution of Maryse Condé's work to this phenomenon, see Sansavior, *Maryse Condé and the Space of Literature*, 8–17.

9   Mireille Rosello, 'Introduction' in Aimé Césaire, *Cahier d'un retour au pays natal*, translated by Mireille Rosello with Annie Pritchard (Newcastle upon Tyne: Bloodaxe Books, 1993), 9–64 (22).

10   For a discussion of the 'post-modern flavor' of this text, see Leah D. Hewitt, *Autobiographical Tightropes: Simone de Beauvoir, Nathalie Sarraute, Marguerite Duras, Monique Wittig, and Maryse Condé* (Lincoln, NE: University of Nebraska Press, 1990), 167.

11   For a stimulating discussion of these 'outmoded' notions, see Alain Robbe-Grillet, 'Sur quelques notions périmées' in *Pour un nouveau roman* (Paris: Les Éditions de Minuit, 1961), 25–44.

12   Léon-Gontran Damas, 'Solde', *Pigments* (Paris: Présence Africaine, 1962).

13   For feminist critique of Fanon's arguments, see for example, Gwen Bergner, 'Who Is That Masked Woman? or, The Role of Gender in Fanon's *Black Skin, White Masks*', *Publications of the Modern Language Association* 110 (1995), 75–88; Lola Young, 'Missing Persons: Fantasizing Black Women in Black Skin, White Masks' in *The Fact of Blackness: Frantz Fanon and Visual Representation*, edited by Alan Read (Seattle, WA: Bay Press; London: Institute of Contemporary Arts, 1996), 86–101; Rey Chow, 'The Politics of Admittance: Female Sexual Agency, Miscegenation, and the Formation of Community in Frantz Fanon' in *Frantz Fanon: Critical Perspectives*, edited by Anthony C. Alessandrini (London and New York: Routledge, 1999), 34–56; T. Denean Sharpley-Whiting, 'Fanon and Capécia' in *Frantz Fanon: Critical Perspectives*, 57–74; Clarisse Zimra, 'Daughters of Mayotte, Sons of Frantz: The Unrequited Self in Caribbean Literature' in *An Introduction to Caribbean Francophone Writing: Guadeloupe and Martinique*, edited by Sam Haigh (Oxford and New York: Berg, 1999), 177–94.

14   Jean-Paul Sartre, 'Dirty Hands' in *No Exit and Three Other Plays*, translated by Stuart Gilbert and Lionel Abel (New York: Vintage, 1989), 240.

Postcolonial Literary History and the Concealed Totality of Life

Eli Park Sorensen

Abstract:

This article attempts to explore some current theoretical problems within the field of postcolonial studies. In particular, I address Ato Quayson's recent complaint that postcolonial theorists generally have failed to 'provide a persuasive account of literature *and* history simultaneously', a problem which I link to what I see as the field's theoretical obsession with the concept of 'representation'; I argue that the field's disciplinary ambition to represent, authoritatively, the postcolonial per se necessarily but also problematically circumscribes and limits its relation to discourses of historical representation and literary representation. On an aesthetic level, this problematic is expressed through postcolonial studies' troubled relationship with literary realism as an aesthetic form. In a wider perspective, I connect the field's disparagement of literary realism with Lazarus's notion of the 'postcolonial unconscious', i.e. postcolonial studies' failure to grasp and address some of the deeper global-political contradictions.

Keywords: postcolonial theory, history, literature, utopia, Caryl Phillips

Introduction

In the article 'The Sighs of History', Ato Quayson looks at some current discussions of the continuing relevance of postcolonial studies, arguing that 'perhaps the most significant accusation that has persistently been made is the failure of postcolonialism to provide a proper account of history'.[1] Commenting specifically on an article by Ann Laura Stoler[2] — in which she claims that postcolonial studies currently suffers from a sense of apathy due to a lack of

Paragraph 37.2 (2014): 235–253
DOI: 10.3366/para.2014.0124
© Edinburgh University Press
www.euppublishing.com/para

a proper understanding of history—Quayson proceeds to address the relation of postcolonialism to *literary* history, an inquiry which, as he insists, is 'not (...) inappropriate' since 'all the key early postcolonial theorists were based in literature departments' (360).[3] More specifically, Quayson argues that one of the main reasons why postcolonial studies has persistently been accused of failing to provide a proper understanding of history is due to the field's disciplinary nature, developing from literary studies but quickly moving on to wider interdisciplinary concerns.[4] Yet despite the field's interdisciplinary aspirations, Quayson writes, 'the question of the meaning of history (...) was lodged within distinctive disciplinary domains' (362), thus failing adequately to bridge the disciplinary differences between literary history and the writing of history proper.

One of the consequences of this trajectory, Quayson proposes, is that 'postcolonial theory did not manage to provide a persuasive account of literature *and* history simultaneously' (362).[5] On the one hand, there was the tendency to focus heavily on discursive ensembles by which texts alone came to illuminate history; on the other hand, Quayson writes, when a critic such as Robert Young—in his monumental *Postcolonialism: An Historical Introduction*—looked at history, 'it was as a postcolonial literary critic writing about history but not about literature' (362).[6] Postcolonial studies thus, according to Quayson, never quite seemed to get the balance right between analyses of literary works per se, discussions of history, and accounts of literary history — switching forth and back between grand claims about world history, global politics, and minute literary analyses. In the following, I explore this alleged imbalance by considering some of the current theoretical concerns within postcolonial studies, the field's relationship to literary texts, and subsequently discussing—via Caryl Phillips's novel *A Distant Shore*—literary realism as the 'political unconscious' of postcolonial studies.[7] The realist dynamic of Phillips's novel, I argue, may serve as an example of what can be seen—more generally—as literature's political-aesthetic potential that has too often been overlooked in postcolonial studies. The field has had surprisingly few positive things to say about literary realism—partly, I believe, because a major concern within postcolonial studies has been that of a critique of the concept of representation.[8] What sustains this theoretical obsession, I argue, is a disciplinary ambition to *represent*—authoritatively—the postcolonial; postcolonialism as a historical phenomenon and as an idea, a concept. It is this disciplinary ambition, I argue, which is challenged by the presence of literary realism.

Postcolonial Studies and Literary History

In what is perhaps one of the most authoritative recent accounts of Anglophone postcolonial literary history, *Colonial and Postcolonial Literature*, Elleke Boehmer outlines a trajectory according to which early postcolonial writers 'tended to identify with a nationalist narrative and to endorse the need for communal solidarity'.[9] Subsequently, Boehmer writes, 'from the late 1980s and into the twenty-first century many writers' geographical and cultural affiliations became more divided, displaced, and uncertain' (*CPL*, 225). In the latter phase, Boehmer continues, the typical postcolonial writer is often a cultural traveller, cosmopolitan in orientation, working 'within the precincts of the Western metropolis while at the same time retaining thematic and/or political connections with a national, ethnic, or regional background' (*CPL*, 227).

It was during the same period — the 1980s, and especially the late 1980s — that postcolonial studies rose to academic prominence, a period that Neil Lazarus, in the book *Resistance in Postcolonial Africa*, has labelled 'the mourning after', which more specifically refers to the widespread disillusionment — with politics, leadership, ideals, communities, independence, democracy, freedom, prosperity and so on — that followed in many countries after liberation.[10] Emerging as a — largely theoretical — response to this historical crisis, the field of postcolonial studies in many ways distanced itself from the ensuing disillusionment by articulating a set of imperatives, which grew bolder and more self-confident as the field gained academic acceptance. At times, postcolonial studies created the impression that colonialism and its legacies could be countered effectively solely by means of textual strategies of dismantling, subverting, disconnecting and deconstructing.

As Boehmer points out in her literary history, many of the themes in the latter phase of postcolonial literature overlap neatly with the theoretical ambitions of postcolonial studies. She writes:

In the western academy and liberal literary establishments, poly-cultural 'translated writing' (. . .) is now widely accepted as one of *the* oppositional, anti-authoritarian literatures or textual strategies of our time (. . .). That this should be so is not too surprising. The minglings of migrant writing accord well with political and critical agendas in western universities (. . .). Its heterogeneity symbolizes the kind of integration and absence of fusty provinciality that, on a cultural level at least, many critics and opinion-makers seek to promote. (*CPL*, 229)

Echoing arguments made by Timothy Brennan, as well as several others,[11] Boehmer suggests that there exists an 'agreement between the writing and the criticism' — which is partly due to location, since both critics and writers 'are situated in the increasingly more heteroglot yet still hegemonic western (or northern) metropolis. Critics therefore feel able to identify with migrant writing because they occupy more or less the same cosmopolitan sphere as its authors' (*CPL*, 229).[12]

Underneath this 'acceptance' of what constitutes '*the* oppositional, anti-authoritarian literatures or textual strategies of our time', at least in a postcolonial perspective — according to which there now allegedly exists an 'agreement' between theory and literature[13] — Boehmer traces a rather a different narrative of retreat, disillusionment and failure, one that indirectly recalls the historical crisis from which postcolonial studies as an academic field arose:

> the emergence of migrant literature in many cases represents a geographic, cultural, and political retreat by writers from the new but ailing nations of the post-colonial world 'back' to the old metropolis. The literatures are a product of that retreat; they are marked by disillusionment, its turn from the political to the aesthetic as a zone of imaginative transformation (. . .). In much of the once-colonized world, decolonization in fact produced few changes: power hierarchies were maintained, the values of former colonizers remained influential (. . .). The practical response by many writers to what Fanon called 'the farce of national independence' has been to seek refuge (. . .) in less repressive and richer places in the world. (*CPL*, 230–1)[14]

An even more forceful and critical exposition of this narrative is provided by Benita Parry who in her book *Postcolonial Studies: A Materialist Critique* argues — with reference to the more enthusiastic approach to the merits of 'poly-cultural' writing endorsed by Bhabha and others — that 'those infatuated by the liberatory effects of dispersion do not address the material and existential conditions of the relocated communities', while leaving 'in obscurity the vast and vastly impoverished populations who cannot and might not choose to migrate'.[15]

While Parry's materialist critique is an important one, John McLeod argues, in an article addressing this specific passage, that: 'Parry is in danger of devaluing or jettisoning new modes of innovative thought which may not be as remote from the "grim prose" of the subaltern lives with which she is concerned'.[16] One may of course develop a more pessimistic view of the qualities of 'poly-cultural' writing, or include other kinds of literatures, perhaps more materialist-oriented in nature, instead of searching for oppositional and anti-authoritarian textual strategies in the same cosmopolitan texts over and over again. This is no doubt a worthwhile effort, but while Bhabha and others may tend to fetishize and exaggerate the liberatory effects of diasporic thought and experience, and by implication cosmopolitan-oriented, 'poly-cultural' texts,[17] Parry's position—seeking out the more negative and tragic history of dispersal, transit and the unhomely[18]—equally seems to illustrate Quayson's point that postcolonial studies has failed to provide a persuasive account of literature and history simultaneously. That is to say, one may argue that both positions—Bhabha's as well as Parry's—operate to some extent with a particular theoretical-historical framework in connexion with which the potential of literary texts is simply limited to expressions of (to use Boehmer's wording) 'agreement' or 'disagreement'.

Postcolonial Studies and the Question of Representation

Crucial to Quayson's objections about postcolonial literary history—the failure to 'provide a persuasive account of literature *and* history simultaneously' (362) due to its disciplinary origins and interdisciplinary aspirations—is, I believe, an issue which Neil Lazarus pertinently addresses in his recent book *The Postcolonial Unconscious* (2011), namely that of *representation*. Questions like 'who is speaking?' and 'of and for whom?' make 'representation', according to Lazarus, 'perhaps the single most fraught and contentious term within postcolonial studies' (*PU*, 114). 'It would not be too much to suggest', Lazarus claims, 'that one defining gesture of scholarship in the field has consisted precisely in its critique of *a specific set of representations*' (*PU*, 114), one that begins with Edward Said's notion of 'Orientalism', and continues throughout all major phases of postcolonial theory. Lazarus elaborates:

in the consolidation of postcolonial studies in the 1980s and 1990s, the signature critique of colonialist (mis-)representation tended to broaden and flatten out. The struggle *over representations* gave way to the struggle *against representation* itself, on the ground that the desire to speak *for, of*, or even *about* others was always shadowed by a secretly authoritarian aspiration. The theoretical resort has then often been to a consideration of difference under the rubric of *incommensurability*. (*PU*, 19)

Lazarus goes on to make a persuasive case demonstrating that 'the vast majority of "postcolonial" literary writing' (*PU*, 19) in fact points in the opposite direction of 'incommensurability', namely towards a 'deep-seated affinity and community, across and athwart the "international division of labour"' (*PU*, 19). What interests me particularly in this context is the argument that postcolonial theory eventually developed a sustained infatuation with a 'struggle against representation itself'. More or less all the classic texts in postcolonial studies — besides Said's *Orientalism*, one could mention Spivak's 'Can the Subaltern Speak?', Bhabha's essays in *The Location of Culture*, as well as *The Empire Writes Back* by Ashcroft, Griffith and Tiffin — were crucially centred around ideas of critically questioning concepts of representation, albeit in different ways.

In a more narrow context, it is this 'struggle against representation itself' which, at least partly I believe, may help us understand some of the implications of Quayson's objection — i.e. the difficult balancing of the literary and the historical in postcolonial studies. What I am suggesting is that the 'theoretical resort' within the field of postcolonial studies in a different register reflects a disciplinary striving to become a representative discourse in its own right — that is, embodying a desire to speak for, of and about the postcolonial per se; a discourse defined as one that struggles against all (other) representations (and, of course, often self-critically its own theoretical assumptions). This disciplinary ambition is furthermore crucial, I believe, in an attempt to elaborate upon Boehmer's observation regarding 'agreement' in the field between theory and literature. For the kind of texts that 'accord well' with postcolonial studies — defined here, for the sake of the argument, simply as a theoretical perspective oriented towards incommensurability as an aesthetic and political norm — are texts that generally lend themselves to questions about their own representativity through textual strategies of difference, hybridity, the in-between, catachresis, un-representativity and, of course, incommensurability. Conversely, as Ulka Anjaria pertinently observes, there is a 'theoretical suspicion of any mode of representation that claims to be mimetic or to represent reality accurately'.[19] The history of postcolonial literary representation in itself — that is, as a *literary* representation and not, say, an agreeable or disagreeable expression of postcolonial theoretical discourse — has, as Quayson indicates, too often been given scant recognition. There are some significant consequences following this tendency, which I address in the remainder of this article.

The Utopian-Political Project of Literature

'Works from the independence period', Nicholas Brown argues in his book *Utopian Generations*, 'no matter how complex, are perpetually submitted to a hermeneutic that mines them for primarily ethnographic and sometimes historical evidence'.[20] A relevant observation notwithstanding, I would argue that it primarily relates to a particular kind of text, or texts that would seem to invite a particular reading, namely those striving to be mimetic; that is, the texts which do not 'accord well' with the above-mentioned postcolonial theoretical perspective. Generally, there are — to oversimplify somewhat, again for the sake of the argument — only a limited number of 'orthodox' ways of reading literary texts within a postcolonial perspective; those readings in which the texts aesthetically and politically 'accord well' with postcolonial studies (typically, so-called self-reflexive, 'resistant' texts); those readings in which the texts are transformed into historical or ethnographic documents (typically, 'mimetically naïve' texts); and finally, an unfortunate category of texts read as aesthetically and politically reactionary.

Regarding the second category of texts — texts generally read *literally* within the field of postcolonial studies — Brown argues that it constitutes an act of hermeneutic violence which, however benevolent and well-intentioned it may seem, is far from innocent: 'it is not merely a blindness but a refusal of the properly eidaesthetic project of postcolonial literature, a refusal to recognize its appropriation of the problem of the absolute, understood explicitly (...) as the social totality' (*UG*, 21).[21] In an ambitious attempt to remap postcolonial literature in a larger historical-materialist perspective, Brown focuses on the notion of 'the eidaesthetic project', derived from German Romantic philosophy, and more specifically readings by Jean-Luc Nancy and Philippe Lacoue-Labarthe of German Romanticism and Friedrich Schlegel's philosophical fragments in *L'Absolu littéraire* (*The Literary Absolute*) from 1978.[22] According to the latter, what characterizes literature in the modern sense is its utopian 'eidaesthetic' vocation, which refers to a conjunction of the philosophical and aesthetic impulses to resolve the antinomies of the world — the sublime reconciliation of the subject and object, the rift between phenomenon and noumenon. But literature, as a romantic-utopian eidaesthetic philosophico-artistic hybrid, eventually 'fails', culminating with modernism which — Brown follows Lukács here — ends up mystifying and ultimately reifying the ambition to overcome the antinomies of capitalism.[23] Furthermore, with modernism literature becomes depoliticized; postmodernism (or the epoch of contemporary western literature) subsequently constitutes, according to Brown, a second 'failure'.

All this, however, falls out very differently regarding the emergence of postcolonial literature, which, Brown argues, rediscovers the original romantic-utopian eidaesthetic vocation, albeit from a different position within the global order. Echoing the epochal lines in Boehmer's literary history, Brown describes the early postcolonial literary texts — texts written during and in the immediate aftermath of liberation — as profoundly utopian, which eventually were replaced by literatures of disillusionment, when the revolutionary dreams and hopes failed to materialize. At this apparent dead-end stage of postcolonial literature, Brown writes, the 'eidaesthetic vocation' as a utopian project 'reappears with the emergence of theory' (*UG*, 24), which thus becomes the true inheritor of the eidaesthetic project.[24] The emergence of theory in the 1960s is according to Brown intimately connected to postcolonial experience — in fact so much so that 'all theory', Brown argues, 'is postcolonial theory' (*UG*, 24).[25]

Brown's trajectory vitally re-orients us back to the utopian-political project of literature, although perhaps also too hastily writes off its continued relevance during the post-independence period in his efforts to identify theory — and more specifically *postcolonial* theory — as the legitimate heir and custodian of this legacy. Neil Lazarus argues that the term 'postcolonial' was originally — during the 1970s — a 'periodising term, an historical and not an ideological term' (*PU*, 11). With Bhabha and others — during the 1980s and 1990s — the term 'postcolonial' gradually starts to designate a set of theoretical imperatives, which are notably 'post-Marxist' or even 'post-modern' in orientation (*PU*, 12). It is this change to which Lazarus's book title refers — the 'postcolonial unconscious', a notion he derives from Jameson's political unconscious.[26] According to Lazarus, one of the most fundamental assumptions of postcolonial studies is that Marxism as a political horizon has become obsolete in the age of globalized capitalism — even though some of the main problems that defined the aims and objectives of Marxism have largely remained as vital as ever: 'developments in the first decade of our new century (...) have exposed the contradictions of this established postcolonial understanding to stark and unforgiving light' (*PU*, 15)[27] — hence, the term 'postcolonial unconscious'. To Lazarus, the 'established postcolonial understanding' — or the institutionalized field of postcolonial studies — has betrayed the legacy of the utopian-political, eidaesthetic project.

Literary Realism and the Postcolonial Unconscious

In *The Postcolonial Unconscious*, Lazarus incorporates an article published previously in different versions, called 'The Politics of Postcolonial Modernism'. The article-version from 2005 outlines the contours of a postcolonial modernist poetics, which — although being aware of the more problematic aspects of modernism — refuses to accept Brown's definition of modernism as literature's 'failure'. In fact, Lazarus wants to insist on

the *ongoing* criticality of modernist literary practice. I am interested in work by contemporary writers (including 'postcolonial' ones), which is (still), arguably, illuminated by recognizably modernist protocols and procedures. (...) [W]e cannot proceed without a theory responsive simultaneously to the notional indispensability and the practical achievement of what, basing myself on Adorno's investigation of the 'Kafka-effect' (...), I will call 'disconsolation' in and through literature.[28]

In the much-expanded book-chapter from 2011, Lazarus maintains this anti-institutional modernist poetics of an aesthetic mode of writing 'that resists the accommodationism of what has been canonised as modernism and that does what at least *some* modernist work has done from the outset: namely, says "no"; refuses integration, resolution, consolation, comfort; protests and criticises' (*PU*, 31). To be slightly polemical, one might argue that Lazarus's staunch modernist poetics in many ways sounds familiar to the position which he — elsewhere in the same book — criticized for being overtly obsessed with the notion of 'incommensurability' (whereas, as Lazarus himself goes on to demonstrate, the 'vast majority' of postcolonial literary writings points in a rather different direction). Perhaps this is why he adds to the book-version from 2011 a brief paragraph on literary realism:

Just before turning to poetry, however, let me note in passing my conviction that we ought, today, to begin to redress a long-standing imbalance in postcolonial literary studies by focusing anew on realist writing. The point is that, inasmuch as the dominant aesthetic dispositions in postcolonial literary studies have from the outset reflected those in post-structuralist theory generally, the categorical disparagement of realism in the latter field has tended to receive a dutiful — if wholly unjustified and unjustifiable — echo in the former. (. . .) [T]here is no good reason for scholars in postcolonial studies to hang on to this dogma today. (*PU*, 82)

Intriguingly, neither the materialist critique outlined by Lazarus — which at least acknowledges the unjustified 'categorical disparagement of realism' — nor indeed the poststructuralist-oriented postcolonial critique have engaged in a serious discussion of the aesthetic-formal potential of realism as a legitimate postcolonial literary mode.[29] Often, as Bruce Robbins has pointed out, critics use a notion of '"naïve realism" as a negative or scapegoat term that a given author, text, period, or genre can be shown to rise sophisticatedly and self-consciously above'.[30] Underneath this circumscribed notion of realism one finds a problematic equation of postcolonial radicalism and literary form. According to David Carter, postcolonial criticism operates with a politicized aesthetic hierarchy according to which realism 'presents a dull and resistant surface to the postcolonial critic'.[31] This dull, resistant surface of realism, it is argued by critics, fails to register and capture the cultural hybridity that one finds in allegedly progressive postcolonial texts. In the context of the British migrant novel, Dominic Head has, however, questioned the tendency to equate cultural hybridity with anti-realist modes, observing that

cultural hybridity is commonly (and erroneously) perceived to go hand-in-glove with overtly experimental forms. In such a view, you either have a startlingly innovative style *and* a rapturous presentation of multicultural energies, or you have neither. Rushdie's exuberant magic realism is thus sometimes seen to exemplify the kind of formal reinvigoration of the novel in Britain that the postcolonial era makes possible. There are certainly grounds for seeing particular instances of formal innovation in this light. However, such an easy equation between experiment and cultural hybridity can imply a simple opposition between experiment and tradition that is inappropriate, with traditional realism coming to embody a reactionary conservatism.[32]

Critical of Head's argument outlined in the quote above, Alistair Cormack argues that Head is making a point that is 'essentially content-led: for him, the radical nature of postcolonial subject matter is transmitted to the reader irrespective of the formal strategies employed by the writer'.[33] Cormack's argument is — once again set against the background of a caricatured version of realism — that 'cultural hybridity has a formal as well as a thematic register; to depict Britain's new hybrid society through realism is not the same as to depict it through other representational modes'. The underlying premiss is here that realist form per se cannot convey 'the radical nature of postcolonial subject matter'. Discussing Monica Ali's novel *Brick Lane* (2003), Cormack argues that the form of the novel becomes radical when it 'ceases to be traditional, because it is called upon to depict this new social juncture; the form's limits become visible, as do the presumptions by which it works' (696). In other words, although Monica Ali's novel form is largely realist, Cormack insists that it only becomes relevant during those brief moments it ceases to be realist. The above example is just one among many — which in a more general perspective indicates an inability or unwillingness to read literary realism within a postcolonial perspective. One is tempted to say that the true aesthetic correlative of the postcolonial unconscious is postcolonial literary realism.

In *The Political Unconscious* — from which, as has been noted, Lazarus derives his notion of the 'postcolonial unconscious' — Fredric Jameson reflected critically on the tendency among contemporary theorists to 'rewrite selected texts from the past (. . .) in terms of a modernist (or more properly post-modernist) conception of language' (2). Often, Jameson continues, such theoretical approaches 'construct a straw man (. . .) — variously called the "readerly" or the "realistic" or the "referential" text — over against which the essential term — the "writerly" or modernist or "open" text (. . .) — is defined and with which it is seen as a decisive break' (2). To modern, western readers, Jameson argues, there is something slightly embarrassing, something 'outmoded', about literary realism — an embarrassment which in Jameson's view comes down to the issue of politics, and more specifically politics related to the history of imperialism and colonialism, as he writes in the controversial essay 'Third-World Literature in the Era of Multinational Capitalism': 'our want of sympathy for these often unmodern third-world texts is itself frequently but a disguise for some deeper fear of the affluent about the way people actually live in other parts of the world'.[34] Elsewhere, Jameson argues in the essay 'Modernism and Imperialism' that 'modernist representation emerges' in a situation 'where the mapping of the new imperial world system becomes impossible, since the colonized other (. . .) has become invisible'.[35] The political-aesthetic aspiration — what Georg Lukács formulated as the novel form's attempt to 'uncover and construct the concealed totality of life',[36] or what Brown labelled the postcolonial eidaesthetic itinerary — subsequently becomes incommensurable with 'the lived experience of our private existences' (69), as Jameson — with a nod towards his thesis in *The Political Unconscious* — writes in the 'Third-World' essay. It is the 'different ratio of the political to the personal', Jameson writes, 'which makes such texts [postcolonial realist texts] alien to us at first approach, and consequently, resistant to our conventional western habits of reading' (69). Lazarus's argument about the postcolonial unconscious — the transformation of the meaning of the 'postcolonial' from a historical concept to a theoretical norm, one that is accompanied by the conviction that a new world order of globalized capitalism has made the Marxist political vocabulary useless — is a development of Jameson's original thesis, albeit without the latter's *aesthetic* reflections on the temporalities of form, and more specifically the *perceived* anachronism of literary realism. My argument here is that the 'disparagement of realism' in postcolonial studies is far from innocent; the inability to say anything serious about realism is, I argue, intimately related to the problematic which Lazarus identifies as the postcolonial unconscious. Literary realism as a symptom of the postcolonial unconscious — that is, read through a postcolonial perspective — thus constitutes an unwelcome reminder on an aesthetic level of the political problems that postcolonial studies promised but ultimately failed to solve, despite the field's interdisciplinary ambitions.

The Concealed Totality of Life

There is a concrete reality that resonates deep within this notion of literary realism as a symptom of the postcolonial unconscious, and it is one that I want to address briefly in conclusion by turning to a contemporary novel, *A Distant Shore* (2003) by the Caribbean-born British novelist Caryl Phillips. The novel narrates the story of a very concrete experience of uprooting and dislocation, but also — in a more meta-theoretical perspective that relates to the issues I have attempted to address in this article — reads like an allegory of the trajectory of postcolonial studies as such. I choose this novel partly because it often figures in postcolonial studies as one of those texts that Boehmer would (and indeed does) identify as a novel that 'agrees' with postcolonial theory, while the potential of the text's realist form has rarely — if ever — been discussed thoroughly. Phillips's novels and essays have generally focused on typical postcolonial themes, including slavery, diaspora, colonization, post-independence, and black identity in British history — thus an oeuvre that corresponds well with Boehmer's argument about the overlap between postcolonial writing and criticism. As Timothy Bewes pertinently has observed, 'Caryl Phillips seems like a gift for readers and critics interested in the theme of black "diaspora" in contemporary literature'. His work, Bewes suggests, 'fits the postcolonial narrative of a theorist such as Homi Bhabha, just as he does—almost unbearably neatly—the "black Atlantic" narrative of Paul Gilroy'.[37]

A Distant Shore tells the story of two interconnected lives, the retired music teacher Dorothy Jones, and the 30-year-old African refugee Solomon Bartholomew. At the beginning of the novel, Dorothy has recently moved to Stoneleigh, a new property development estate in northern England, where she attempts to start a new life, while trying to leave behind memories of a painful past. Her life seems to take a positive turn when she begins a discreet but promising friendship with her neighbour, the African refugee Solomon. In the remaining parts, we retrospectively hear about Dorothy's and Solomon's haunting pasts, the agonizing personal stories that condition and frame their encounter in the present. The traumatic and extremely violent refugee narrative that Solomon carries with him contrasts radically with Dorothy's quotidian story of domestic disappointment, abandonment and rejection, but in both cases we get a sense of deep isolation and un-belonging, albeit in different ways. The novel gives us no more, however, than a fleeting glimpse of what could have been a common future—Solomon being brutally killed by racist skinheads, while Dorothy consequently suffers a mental breakdown from which she never recovers. The novel bleakly ends with Dorothy being transferred to a psychiatric hospital.

These are the main narrative strands in a novel that consists of many intricately interwoven stories. Yet, in another sense it is a novel that reads like so many attempts to narrate a larger story; a narrative permanently in the mode of preparing itself to narrate its story, one that—as a consequence of these narrative run-ups—remains conspicuously absent. As for Dorothy's life narrative, there is, as she puts it, not much to say: it is a story that 'contains the single word, abandonment' (203). Abandoned by her husband—after a dull, loveless marriage—Dorothy embarks on a series of quietly disastrous affairs with men who share Dorothy's company largely because there is no one else around. Everything around Dorothy seems deliberately dragged down to a level of the absolutely mundane; a world marred by acute boredom, pervasive insignificance and ubiquitous depression. Conversely, in the case of Solomon's life narrative, there is almost too much to relate. Solomon's overdetermined past is one that contains adventurous anecdotes of heroic deeds as well as betrayal and cowardice; stories about his time as a soldier in a West-African militant faction rebelling against a corrupt political regime; testimonies of unspeakable horrors and unpunished acts of atrocities. And yet, for all its raw power and force, Solomon's narrative is one that remains profoundly un-narratable, except in isolation, detached and securely demarcated from his present life. 'If I do not share my story, then I have only this one year to my life. I am a one-year-old man who walks with heavy steps. I am a man burdened with hidden history' (300), Solomon reflects, hoping that he might tell his story to Dorothy some day. Soon after, however, Solomon dies — as a 'one-year-old man' — and with him, of course, his hidden history. Although the hopeful friendship between Dorothy and Solomon — which constitutes the backbone of the novel's plot — points towards the contours of a larger narrative, it is an impulse already quenched at the end of the first part of the novel, which brings the news of Solomon's horrid death at the hands of a local racist gang.[38]

Here, the transformation of the figure of Solomon — from postcolonial liberation fighter to history-less migrant — reads like a critical comment upon that problematic which Lazarus identified as the postcolonial unconscious; in a wider sense, of course, it reads like an allegory of the trajectory of postcolonial studies as such. The novel's laborious narrative furthermore addresses in a very literal sense what Lazarus saw as the postcolonial obsession with 'the struggle against representation itself'; yet it also strives to overcome this 'meaning loss' of the metropolis (the melancholic life of Dorothy), above all by insisting on bringing to the surface — or to that distant shore — the 'invisible' narrative of the colonized other, to paraphrase Jameson, even if this narrative remains forever locked away in the political unconscious, unable to break through the reification of contemporary provincial English life. It is nonetheless precisely the novel's schizophrenic narrative realist dynamic — Dorothy's history of post-war England, and Solomon's hidden postcolonial history, two narratives clinically kept apart except for a few precious encounters — that sends us back, yet again, to the unresolved problematic of the subject–object antinomy, or in Lazarus's words the postcolonial unconscious, which here more concretely means the political-aesthetic aspiration of the novel's realist form; in Lukács's words, to 'uncover and construct the concealed totality of life' (60). That this is the trajectory of a literary history which by now has largely become unfamiliar to us — as Quayson intimates — is indirectly reflected in what Boehmer identified as the 'agreement' between postcolonial theory and writing today. Within this 'agreeable' relationship, the political–aesthetic impulse of literary realism is typically reduced to a 'straw man' — all the while it continues to haunt the postcolonial unconscious.

In this article, I have attempted to address some current theoretical problems within the field of postcolonial studies. I began with Ato Quayson's complaint that postcolonial theorists generally have failed to 'provide a persuasive account of literature *and* history simultaneously', a problem which I linked to Boehmer's literary history according to which an 'agreement' exists between theory and the political–aesthetic potential of ('canonized' or 'preferred') postcolonial literary texts. Underpinning this 'agreement', Boehmer outlined the emergence of a cosmopolitan-oriented literature marked by disillusionment, which coincided with the institutional rise of postcolonial studies as an academic field. Lazarus's pertinent discussion of the field's obsession with the problematic of representation — one that eventually developed into a sustained 'struggle against representation itself' — was, I argued, both touching upon the underlying problems following Quayson's concern about postcolonial literary history, *and* Boehmer's argument about the current 'agreement' between theory and literature. Implicit in this 'struggle against representation itself' is, I argued, a disciplinary ambition to represent, authoritatively, the postcolonial per se, an ambition necessarily but also problematically circumscribing the analysis of both history and literary texts. On an aesthetic level, this problematic is expressed through postcolonial studies' troubled relationship with literary realism as an aesthetic form, or an eidaesthetic itinerary, to use Brown's terminology. There is nothing innocent about this postcolonial 'disparagement of realism', I argued, at least not insofar as it constitutes a symptom of a larger problematic, namely the 'postcolonial unconscious', and, in that sense, a narrative of the return of the repressed — unwanted and unwelcome, like Phillips's catastrophic characters.

NOTES

1   Ato Quayson, 'The Sighs of History: Postcolonial Debris and the Question of (Literary) History', *New Literary History* 43 (2012), 359–70 (360); subsequent references in the text.

2   Ann Laura Stoler, 'Imperial Debris: Reflections on Ruins and Ruination', *Cultural Anthropology* 23 (2008), 191–219. In the article, Stoler describes

postcolonial studies as 'overconfident in its analytics and its conceptual vocabulary, too assured of what we presume to know about the principles and practices of empire that remain in an active register' (192).

3 See also the argument that postcolonial studies never managed to move beyond literature departments in Vinaj Lal, 'The Politics of Culture and Knowledge after Postcolonialism: Nine Theses (and a Prologue)', *Continuum: Journal of Media & Cultural Studies* 26 (2012), 191–205 (192).

4 On postcolonial studies and interdisciplinarity, see also Malreddy Pavan Kumar, 'Postcolonialism: Interdisciplinary or Interdiscursive?', *Third World Quarterly* 32:4 (2011), 653–72.

5 Although a number of persuasively argued literary-historical works on postcolonial literatures exists—for example, Nicholas Harrison's *Postcolonial Criticism: History, Theory and the Work of Fiction* (Cambridge: Polity Press, 2003)—Quayson's argument may still be relevant, I believe, on a more general level.

6 Robert J. Young, *Postcolonialism: An Historical Introduction* (Oxford: Oxford University Press, 2006).

7 Caryl Phillips, *A Distant Shore* (London: Secker and Warburg, 2003).

8 Neil Lazarus develops this argument in *The Postcolonial Unconscious*, to which I will return below. See Neil Lazarus, *The Postcolonial Unconscious* (Cambridge: Cambridge University Press, 2011); henceforward referred to as *PU*.

9 Elleke Boehmer, *Colonial and Postcolonial Literature: Migrant Metaphors* (Oxford: Oxford University Press, 2005), 225; henceforward referred to as *CPL*. For similar trajectories of postcolonial literary history, see Robert Fraser, *Lifting the Sentence* (Manchester: Manchester University Press, 2000), and *The Cambridge History of Postcolonial Literature*, edited by Ato Quayson, 2 vols (Cambridge: Cambridge University Press, 2012).

10 Neil Lazarus, *Resistance in Postcolonial African Fiction* (New Haven: Yale University Press, 1990), 1.

11 Timothy Brennan, *At Home in the World: Cosmopolitanism Now* (Cambridge, MA: Harvard University Press, 1997), 425.

12 Here, Boehmer lists writers like Derek Walcott, Salman Rushdie, Jamaica Kincaid, Caryl Phillips, Ben Okri, Nourbese Phillip, Olive Senior, Amitav Ghosh, Nuruddin Farah, and Vikram Seth (*CPL*, 226).

13 See Brennan, *At Home in the World*, 425; *PU*, 22; and Graham Huggan, *The Postcolonial Exotic: Marketing the Margins* (London: Routledge, 2001), viii, for discussions of the 'agreement' between theory and literature in postcolonial studies.

14 'Often retracing the biographical paths of their authors', Boehmer writes, 'novels by (...) Rushdie, Ghosh, Kincaid, Phillips, Okri, Kamila Shamsie, and Bernadine Evaristo, ramify across widely separate geographical, historical, and cultural spaces. They are marked by the pull of conflicting ethics

and philosophies — a potential source of tragedy — and often comically contrasting forms of social behaviour' (*CPL*, 227).

15 Benita Parry, *Postcolonial Studies: A Materialist Critique* (London: Routledge, 2004), 100. Also quoted in John McLeod, 'Diaspora and Utopia: Reading the Recent Work of Paul Gilroy and Caryl Phillips' in *Diasporic Literature and Theory: Where Now?*, edited by Mark Shackleton (Cambridge: Cambridge Scholars Publishing, 2008), 2–17 (4).

16 'Diaspora and Utopia', 4.

17 See Parry's critique of Bhabha's position in the essay 'Signs of the Time', included in *Postcolonial Studies*, 55–74.

18 See here particularly Parry's essay 'Internationalism revisited or in praise of internationalism', included in *Postcolonial Studies*, 93–103.

19 Ulka Anjaria, *Realism in the Twentieth-Century Indian Novel: Colonial Difference and Literary Form* (Cambridge: Cambridge University Press, 2012), 3.

20 Nicholas Brown, *Utopian Generations: The Political Horizon of Twentieth-Century Literature* (Princeton, NJ: Princeton University Press, 2009), 21; henceforward referred to as *UG*. Brown here follows Spivak's discussion in *A Critique of Postcolonial Reason: Toward a History of the Vanishing Present* (Cambridge, MA: Harvard University Press, 1999), 388.

21 For an extended discussion of the particular factors that condition postcolonial modes of reading, see Huggan's *The Postcolonial Exotic: Marketing the Margins*.

22 Philippe Lacoue-Labarthe and Jean-Luc Nancy, *The Literary Absolute: The Theory of Literature in German Romanticism* (New York: State University of New York Press, 1988).

23 See *UG*, 20.

24 For a discussion of the contemporary inheritors of the eidaesthetic project, see *UG*, 173–99.

25 Brown refers, among others, to Lévi–Strauss and the crisis in French anthropology; Derrida's essay 'Structure, Sign, and Play in the Discourse of the Human Sciences' interpreting this crisis; Barthes's African soldier saluting the French flag; and Foucault's announcement of the end of humanism. For similar discussions of the relationship between theory in general and postcolonial experience in particular, see Robert J. Young, *White Mythologies: Writing History and the West* (London: Routledge, 2004), *Postcolonialism: An Historical Introduction*, and Michael Syrotinski, *Deconstruction and the Postcolonial: At the Limits of Theory* (Liverpool: Liverpool University Press, 2007).

26 Fredric Jameson, *The Political Unconscious: Narrative as a Socially Symbolic Act* (London: Routledge, 2002).

27 One could add here Vinaj Lal's critique of postcolonial studies: 'During the three decades that postcolonial studies flourished in the American academy, the United States engaged in rapacious conduct around the world (. . .).

The gist of all this should, in any case, be transparent: before we convince ourselves of a postcolonial fatigue, perhaps we should seriously ask if postcolonial studies travelled as far as is sometimes believed' ('The Politics of Culture and Knowledge after Postcolonialism', 192).

28 Neil Lazarus, 'The Politics of Postcolonial Modernism' in *Postcolonial Studies and Beyond*, edited by Ania Loomba et al. (Durham, NC: Duke University Press, 2005), 423–38 (431). An earlier version appeared in *European Legacy* 7 (2002), 771–82.

29 Recent exceptions here include Anjaria's *Realism in the Twentieth-Century Indian Novel*, and Dave Gunning, 'Ethnicity, Authenticity, and Empathy in the Realist Novel and Its Alternatives', *Contemporary Literature* 53:3 (2012), 779–813.

30 Bruce Robbins, 'Modernism and Literary Realism: Response' in *Realism and Representation: Essays on the Problem of Realism in Relation to Science, Literature and Culture*, edited by George Levine (Madison: Wisconsin University Press, 1993), 225–31 (227).

31 David Carter, 'Tasteless Subjects: Postcolonial Literary Criticism, Realism and the Subject of Taste', *Southern Review* 25 (1992), 292–303 (296).

32 Dominic Head, *The Cambridge Introduction to Modern British Fiction, 1950–2000* (Cambridge: Cambridge University Press, 2002), 172.

33 Alistair Cormack, 'Migration and the Politics of Narrative Form: Realism and the Postcolonial Subject in *Brick Lane*', *Contemporary Literature* 47:4 (2006), 695–721 (696).

34 Fredric Jameson, 'Third-World Literature in the Era of Multinational Capitalism', *Social Text* 15 (1986), 65–88 (66).

35 Fredric Jameson, 'Modernism and Imperialism' in *Nationalism, Colonialism and Literature: Terry Eagleton, Fredric Jameson, Edward W. Said*, edited by Seamus Deane (Minneapolis: University of Minnesota Press, 1990), 43–66 (50). To Jameson, modernist representation is an aesthetic response to a loss of meaning; since 'a significant structural segment of the economic system as a whole is now located elsewhere, beyond the metropolis, outside of the daily life and existential experience of the home country' (50–1).

36 Georg Lukács, *The Theory of the Novel*, translated by Anna Bostock (London: Merlin, 2003), 60.

37 Timothy Bewes, 'Shame, Ventriloquy, and the Problem of the Cliché in Caryl Phillips', *Cultural Critique* 63 (2006), 33–60 (33 and 54). It goes without saying that my concluding remarks on Phillips's novel will in no way be able to address all the aspects this complex novel raises; my reading will only serve as brief, practical example of some of the theoretical issues I have been concerned with during this article. For more comprehensive postcolonial readings of the novel, see in particular Bénédicte Ledent, *Caryl Phillips* (Manchester: Manchester University Press, 2002); the special issue

Moving Worlds 7 (2007); John McLeod, 'Diaspora and Utopia: Reading the Recent Work of Paul Gilroy and Caryl Phillips', and Stephen Clingman, *The Grammar of Identity: Transnational Fiction and the Nature of the Boundary* (Oxford: Oxford University Press, 2009).

38 Along similar lines, albeit in a somewhat different approach, John McLeod reads a 'tentative utopian vision' in Phillips's novel ('Diaspora and Utopia', 13).

Globalization, *mondialisation* and the *immonde* in Contemporary Francophone African Literature

MICHAEL SYROTINSKI

Abstract:

Taking as its theoretical frame of reference Jean-Luc Nancy's distinction between globalization and *mondialisation*, this article explores the relationship between contemporary Africa, the 'world' and the 'literary'. The discussion centres on a number of present-day African novelists, and looks in particular at a controversial recent text by the Cameroonian writer and critic, Patrice Nganang, who is inspired by the work of the well-known theorist of postcolonial Africa, Achille Mbembe. For both writers 'Africa', as a generic point of reference, is seen in terms of a certain genealogy of Africanist thinking, from colonial times through to the contemporary postcolonial era, and the article reflects on what a radical challenge to this genealogy might entail. Using a more phenomenologically oriented reading of *monde* (world) and *immonde* (abject, literally un–world), this rupture could be conceived in terms of the kind of 'epistemological break' that thinkers like Althusser and Foucault introduced into common usage and theoretical currency in contemporary French thought back in the 1960s.

Keywords: globalization, *mondialisation*, *immonde*, postcolonial, literary, post-genocide, decolonization, dis-enclosure

What theory would be most fitting for contemporary Africa when considering its place in today's allegedly 'globalized' world? The question quickly becomes a very crowded one, with an almost infinite number of possible theories, whether anthropological (the work of an anthropologist of popular culture such as Johannes Fabian, or the urban ethnography of Paul Stoller, for example), economic (including sustained critiques of neoliberalism from various perspectives by thinkers such as Célestin Monga, James Ferguson, or Gayatri Spivak),

Paragraph 37.2 (2014): 254–272
DOI: 10.3366/para.2014.0125
© Edinburgh University Press
www.euppublishing.com/para

theological (Jean-Marc Ela, John Mbiti, Fabian Eboussi–Boulaga), and one could go on: theorists of African sociology, politics, environmentalism, technology, history and philosophy, to name but a few, have all been concerned with questions of globalization over the last two decades. Within this purview, and given the economic, political and indeed natural crises which continue to beset Africa, literary theory would seem to be of marginal interest, and literature itself a non-essential indulgence that comes well down the list in any order of priorities. Within this article I would like to make the case and the counter-claim, however, that recent developments in contemporary African literature, and literary theory, are in fact crucial to any reflection upon the question of Africa in a contemporary global context. 'Literary', however, is to be understood here in a broader and more inclusive sense than one might immediately assume, and as we shall see, it is perhaps in itself a 'global' term that might encompass multiple forms of artistic or linguistic invention, and would thus be closer to the imaginative power, the sheer force of creation, that one associates with the poetic.[1] Taken in this broader perspective, 'the literary' as I am using it is less to do with the long history of debates about the respective value or status of the written as it comes to supplant or transform orality in Africa. Nor the more complex versions of this debate and its inherent tensions that tend to dominate and structure postcolonial studies, and which often pit 'textualist' approaches against 'materialist' (often broadly Marxist) theories.

My discussion will centre on a few contemporary writers, and look in particular at a controversial recent text by the Cameroonian novelist and critic, Patrice Nganang, and his adaptation of the ideas of the leading theorist of postcolonial Africa, Achille Mbembe. From his early publications such as *Afriques indociles*, and then most forcefully in his best-known text, *On the Postcolony*, Mbembe has challenged a certain received set of critical assumptions informing Africanist studies, and by implication the way in which 'Africa' as a name and a concept has served as a generic point of reference. I am interested in how we might think of the radical discursive rupture which Mbembe has articulated, and which has been given extensive literary-theoretical expression by Nganang, as a recent manifestation of the kind of the 'epistemological break' that thinkers like Althusser and Foucault first introduced into common usage and theoretical currency back in the 1960s.

One writer and thinker whose work has proved particularly fruitful in rethinking the question of globalization in relation to the literary is the French philosopher, Jean–Luc Nancy.[2] In his 2002 text *La création du monde, ou la mondialisation*,[3] Nancy makes a distinction between two ways in which one can understand the term 'globalization', within the context of a reading of Marx — specifically a Marxist theorization of what it might mean to 'change the world' — and more broadly in relation to religious theories of worldly immanence and transcendence. His reflection turns on a reading of the difference between the English term globalization, and its not quite synonymous French equivalent, *mondialisation*. This difference, often translated rather uncritically, is crucial for Nancy: in his reading, globalization as represented by the globalized economy, exchange value and capitalist accumulation, is seen as a totalizing movement which conceives of the world according to a logic of 'bad infinity' (*CW*, 38). To this, Nancy opposes the world-forming logic of *mondialisation* — as he puts it, 'the world has lost its capacity to "form a world" [*faire monde*]' (*CW*, 34) — which he figures as a creation '*ex nihilo*', and in this respect it is part of Nancy's more wide-ranging 'post-phenomenological' philosophy. 'Creating a world' thus involves a kind of suspension of every previous representation of the world: 'To create the world means: immediately, without delay, reopening each possible struggle for a world, that is, for what must form the opposite of a global injustice against a background of general equivalence' (*CW*, 54). His version of immanence is in contrast both to onto-theological transcendence, and to the mistaken belief that a capitalist globalization operates independently of the transcendental metaphysics out of which it emerged. We might say that it is, in a similar vein to Derrida's deconstructive reading of Heidegger, a mining of onto-theology from within. In many ways, this can be seen as a reformulation of an earlier opposition which Nancy developed in *The Inoperative Community*[4] between Myth (as a kind of totalizing representation of the world, which would be consonant with globalization understood as bad infinity), and Literature (whose interruptive force and meaning is described precisely as a kind of epistemological break, which undoes the synthetic totality of Myth, and is seen as a more fundamental creative act, the creation of a world). How, then, does this notion of interruption, rupture or brokenness manifest itself in recent contemporary African writing?

Broken Glass

I will start out with a quotation from the opening of the novel from 2005, *Verre cassé* (*Broken Glass*) by the well-known Francophone

African writer from Congo-Brazzaville, Alain Mabanckou. Like its sequel, *Mémoires de porc-épic* (2006) (*Memoirs of a porcupine*), it is set in the local community bar, *Le Crédit a voyagé* (*Credit Gone West*), and the opening section immediately brings into play some of the questions about the place of the 'literary' in contemporary Francophone African writing, thereby setting the tone for the rest of the novel:

let's say the boss of the bar Credit Gone West gave me this notebook to fill, he's convinced that I — Broken Glass — can turn out a book, because one day, for a laugh, I told him about this famous writer who drank like a fish, and had to be picked up off the street when he got drunk, which shows you should never joke with the boss, he takes everything literally, when he gave me this notebook he said from the start it was only for him, no one else would read it, and when I asked why he was so set on this notebook, he said he didn't want Credit Gone West just to vanish one day, and added that people in this country have no sense of the importance of memory, that the day when grandmothers reminisced from their deathbeds was gone now, this is the age of the written word, that's all that is left, the spoken word's just black smoke, wild cat's piss, the boss of Credit Gone West doesn't like ready-made phrases like 'in Africa, whenever an old person dies, a library burns', every time he hears that worn-out cliché he gets mad, he'll say 'depends which old person, don't talk crap, I only trust what's written down'[5]

The 'customer' narrator who is asked to produce this book, which has the same title as the book we will subsequently read, writes about the life of the bar, and some of the down-and-outs who frequent it, with an irrepressible inventiveness and verve that is reminiscent of the great Congolese writer Sony Labou Tansi's 1979 novel, *La Vie et demie* (*Life and a Half*, which is alluded to in *Verre cassé*, and is indeed a major point of reference for Achille Mbembe when he talks of the 'life after death' of the African postcolony). From the outset, *Verre cassé* clearly figures the 'shattered' subject of contemporary Africa, and as the narrator finally gets round to his own sorry tale, he reveals himself to be the most 'broken' of all the characters in the novel. The stories of the low-life subjects who populate this novel, though, are narrated in a style that is acutely aware of the place it occupies within a certain African literary history and tradition. The phrase 'whenever an old person dies, a library burns', is of course a reference to the famous saying by Ahmadou Hampâté Ba, expressing the continuing attachment to the indigenous culture and oral tradition from which much African ethno-philosophy takes its cue. Mabanckou's novel — like that of Patrice Nganang, as we shall see later on — is playfully critical of this tradition, and is in fact packed full of intertextual allusions to many classic French and Francophone African texts. Indeed, a large part of his literary strategy is to challenge our notion of what we assume to be literary, to deliberately blur the lines separating the 'literary' and the 'oral' (his literary style is distinctly oral, but in a very contemporary mode), and at the same time to question the distinction between French and African, and the very notion of national ownership of a language and a literary tradition in a complex transnational, globalized world.

The question of the relationship of Francophone 'literature' to the 'world' was brought into sharp focus recently in what has become a landmark statement of intent, the 2007 *littérature-monde* manifesto, which made a series of bold claims to break with the enduring francocentrism of *francophonie*, and thereby to open the way for a radically decentred and transnational French-language literature, which might share the same globalized perspectives and concerns as Anglophone World Literature.[6] Around the same time, the Francophone Cameroonian novelist, Patrice Nganang, wrote an equally radical manifesto, *Manifeste d'une nouvelle littérature africaine: Pour une écriture pré-emptive*, which stands in a contrapuntal negative relation to the affirmative, celebratory tone of the *littérature-monde* manifesto.[7] Nganang's manifesto is in effect a rather provocative indirect challenge to the latter's optimistic transnationalism, and a rallying cry for a new (as he terms it, 'pre-emptive') French-language African literature, in which he makes a claim to a certain worldliness: for him, the defining moment of recent African history, and West/Africa relations, was the Rwandan genocide. According to Nganang, this was the point at which a long tradition of African thinking effectively reached its limit, and the best hope for its rebirth is literature, but literature considered as essentially, profoundly, and necessarily *dissident*. Nganang accuses contemporary African writing and philosophy of not truly confronting the implications of what happened in Rwanda, with the notable exception of Achille Mbembe, whose work marks an explicit rupture with ideologies and prevalent African philosophies of subjectivity. Nganang thus sees within contemporary literature a differently conceived 'worldliness', and a radically new African subjectivity.

Writing in the Wake of Disaster

Nganang's central thesis is that the Rwandan genocide has to be read as symptomatic of a wider *self-destruction* in the context of the history of Francophone Africa. Rather than being a socio–political or historical analysis of the Rwandan genocide, the conditions which made it possible and its aftermath (analyses which many others have undertaken), Nganang implicates not only the West, but more importantly, *what had gone under the name of African philosophy* until that point. He begins with a critique of Africa's belated response to the genocide, which he calls 'a belated ritual that has its origins in the deep-seated guilt of African thinking, which fell asleep at the moment of the catastrophe' (*M*, 25). The most immediate consequence is that African thinking and writing now has to define itself 'as necessarily post-genocide' (27). However, the drama (and 'truth') of the genocide for Nganang lies precisely in the fact that it was not exceptional: not only was it the logical culmination of a series of earlier 'smaller' episodes of genocidal violence that scarred the history of Rwanda, and not only was it merely the latest in a long history of barbaric post-Independence political regimes in Africa — what he calls 'the time of the exception which has become the rule' (27) — but in global historical terms it pales by comparison with far larger-scale crimes against humanity (the systematic slaughter of American Indians, the Holocaust, Cambodia, and so on). Through a cruel irony, the Rwandan genocide, insofar as it becomes part of this broader history of world barbarism, marks the moment when Africa becomes, as Nganang puts it, 'fully human': 'the tragic paradox is that the genocide makes the African fully human' (30). The myth of Africa as different, extraordinary, other (whether positively or negatively conceived) no longer holds: instead the genocide is the moment of Africa's violent entry into 'simple, that is to say flawed, humanity' (30).

The Kantian or Hegelian subject around which most humanist discourses are constructed is thus replaced by the figure of the survivor (33), and this is paradoxically, according to Nganang, a new foundational moment for African philosophy. As he puts it: 'thinking negatively in order to survive is the new gesture which becomes an imperative for philosophy after the genocide, which founds a new humanity, a new subjectivity' (36). In this sense, Rwanda would effectively render obsolete the philosophy of a thinker like Valentin Mudimbe, whose patient archeological uncovering of the historically determined misrepresentations, or 'inventions' of Africa, would appear to have been leading African thinking up a blind alley all along. Naming him explicitly, Nganang implicates Mudimbe when he says: 'even the most patient of African philosophers fell asleep while the dead bodies were adorning his back yard' (40). For him, this underlines 'the inability of [African philosophy] to have foreseen the catastrophe of the genocide, and the sudden appearance of the unthought at its very heart' (40).[8] By contrast, however, Achille Mbembe is said to be the one writer and thinker who reads the 'time' of contemporary Africa not so much as 'a time of the ritual of mourning, rather one of waking up after the genocide: of life after death' (41), whereas for other writers, the genocide was considered to be an 'epiphenomenon', a kind of exceptional and uncharacteristic madness.

It is certainly true that Mbembe's analysis takes this violence as inextricably bound up with the very ontology of the subject in contemporary Africa. In the chapter 'Of *Commandement*' in his best-known text, *On the Postcolony*, Mbembe traces the corruption and violence that is at the heart of many African postcolonial regimes back to the 'founding violence' of the act of imperial conquest. Under colonialism, and the humanism which gave it its moral justification and ideological underpinning, the native African was explicitly excluded from the realm of the human, and belonged to what Mbembe terms 'the grammar of animality'.[9] In other words, the same dynamics that structured the African as a colonial 'animal' still determine the power relations of subjectivity and subjection in the African postcolony, since the African subject is considered ontologically as a 'thing that is nothing', and Mbembe goes on to ask the question: 'What does it mean to do violence to what is nothing?' (174).

These ontological questions take a more overtly political turn in Mbembe's most recent text, *Sortir de la grande nuit*, written in the context of the fiftieth anniversary of the decolonization of much of the African continent. The privileged concept for Mbembe is Jean-Luc Nancy's term 'dis-enclosure' (*déclosion*), which is a neologism used principally by Nancy to re-read Christian motifs in a number of thinkers and literary traditions. For Nancy, as Mbembe points out, this term indicates the act of opening up something that is not only closed, but also enclosed, such as an enclosure. It is thus a profoundly transformative act, that is at the same time a coming into being, or *éclosion* (literally: hatching). It might thus be seen as precisely analogous to the creative and transformative difference between globalization and *mondialisation* in *The Creation of the World*. As Mbembe puts it: 'The idea of *déclosion* includes that of *éclosion*, of an eruption, or advent of something new, of an opening out' (*SGN*, 68). The term *déclosion* is thus adopted by Mbembe as a paronomastic link-word joining together *éclosion*, *déclosion*, and *décolonisation*, connecting Nancy's (post-)phenomenological rethinking of being and the world to the radical political anti-colonialism of Fanon and his successors, in that decolonization is essentially about reclaiming a world, and one's place within the world. This allows for the possibility of a return to the hidden and perhaps neglected creative political force of the *Négritude* philosophy of Léopold Sedar Senghor, whose vision for the future of Africa has, since Independence, been largely discredited as regressive or essentialist, certainly in relation to the more politically uncompromising voices of thinkers such as Césaire and Fanon. It is, however, precisely Senghor's reflection on universalism — that is, how we can think the specificity of Africa in relation to the question of universal humanism — which echoes closely Nancy's conceptualization of 'being-in-common', articulating the singularity of existence as a necessary relationship of sharing, of *partage*. This is how Mbembe brings Fanon and Senghor back together:

In his [Nancy's] eyes, this 'making common' [*mise en commun*] is the basis for the rebirth of the world, and the coming of a mixed universal community, governed by the principle of a sharing of both differences, and of what is unique, and in this respect, open to the whole. In the case of Fanon as in that of Senghor, we are heirs to the whole world. At the same time the world — and thus this legacy — still remain to be created. The world is in creation, as are we too. (*SGN*, 70–1)

The 'poetics' of 'writing Africa' are ultimately at the heart of a very strong political agenda for Mbembe, which he terms 'Afropolitanism':

Afropolitanism is not the same thing as Panafricanism or Negritude. Afropolitanism is a stylistics and a politics, an aesthetics and a certain poetics of the world. It is a way of being in the world which as a principle refuses any identity as victim (...). It also takes a political and cultural position with respect to the nation, to race, and to the question of difference in general. (*SGN*, 232)

Déclosion is thus seen as a means of reactivating the lost energy of decolonization, a means of enabling Africa to free itself from the continuing legacy of colonialism in all its forms, and at the same time to stake a strong and active claim for its place within the contemporary globalized world. Nganang's thesis on 'post-genocide writing' is explicitly aligned with Mbembe's rejection of the two traditions which since *Négritude* have dominated African thinking, that is Marxism in its various guises, and Afrocentrist indigenism. From the perspective of radical political philosophy, Nganang sees the subject as perpetually stuck in a relationship of victimization, projecting everything negative on to colonialism, and seeing him/herself as Other, in Hegelian terms:

'the external origins of a mass extermination predetermined by the dichotomies of Belgian colonialism, and the long genocidal hand of France' (*M*, 45). For him, as for Mbembe, this effectively stymies the possibility of an unconditional responsibility for autonomy. Indigenism or nativism, on the other hand, can only be founded on essentialism, and as Nganang rightly says, it was precisely this essentialist thinking, 'identitarian thinking' (45) which informed the racialism motivating the genocide. It revealed at the same time the profound historical and ideological complicity linking rationalism with racialism: 'it was the very foundation of rationality that was shaken. Rwanda is without a doubt the graveyard of negritude, as well as of all of its conceptual corollaries' (46). Mbembe's unique status as a post-genocide writer comes precisely from his willingness to position himself specifically within the space left as a result of the wreckage of the two traditions of radicalism and nativism: 'We can say then that Mbembe's thought, by asking the question of the sovereignty of the subject in its chaos, discovers the wisdom of African philosophy in its lack, close by to danger, on the border with death, for sure, but also in the negation of both of these' (*M*, 52).

Literature and the *im-monde*

As we saw earlier, this negative foundational moment is what provides Nganang in his *Manifeste* with the impetus for a new (what he calls 'pre-emptive') African literature: a certain African philosophy died in Rwanda, and can only be reborn in literature, but a literature that is characterized by its essential dissidence (perpetual dissidence thus functions as a sort of insurance policy preventing it from falling back into the same old traps, or the same old structures and complicities). For him this renewed subjectivity is not to be found in the old discredited philosophies, but by venturing deep into the heart of contemporary urban Africa (for which his shorthand term is 'la rue' [the street]). This is not so much the expression of a commitment to write in a populist vein, or to place his finger on an authentically popular 'pulse', but he characterizes this literature as an incessant, urgent, anxious vigilance, informed by a knowing wisdom about what it means to live — most often to survive — in the African postcolony, but also in terms of a particular linguistic inventiveness: 'we know how offhand, informal and inventive the language of the street is in Africa' (*M*, 11). In the second half of his *Manifeste*, he sketches out an aesthetics of contemporary African literature, distancing himself from more conventional textual analysis, or from discussions of literature in terms of its status as sociological or historical document (whether in its representational or allegorical mode), but elevates literature instead to a more philosophically pre-eminent position, giving it what one could call a metaphysical function, as the development of an *idea*: 'what we mean by idea is making "our own" street language the place where one begins to ask questions and to philosophize' (16). Nganang outlines some of the formal characteristics of this new 'philosophical' literature (literature is the expression of a 'pre-visionary' kind of truth; it is marked by chiasmic, ironic forms; and it is tragic in its dimensions), and then describes a number of broad categories (the literature of dictatorship, the literature of emigration, the literature of 'detritus'), but it is really this last category which is truly the place where Nganang sees the 'post-genocidal African subject' tentatively taking shape. It is within this context that he mentions the novels of Alain Mabanckou, and the opening sequence quoted above perhaps now comes into sharper focus. He also refers explicitly to his own fiction-writing, and I will turn briefly to one of his novels, perhaps the best known, *Temps de chien* (*Dog Days: An Animal Chronicle*).

Both Mabanckou and Nganang's novels are very much novels of 'la rue': the language is a rich, earthy, Africanized French (in the manner of Yambo Ouologuem, Ahmadou Kourouma, or Sony Labou Tansi), and the characters all seem to be part of the 'detritus' that characterizes the human-as-survivor, but they also explicitly pose the question of the subject as a kind of *post-human* subject, telling their stories from the point of view of two animal narrators. These narrators are both presented as wise, affectionate and forgiving observers of human nature, however, constantly thinking about the meaning of the human as such, and forever questioning the activities and behaviours of the many different characters they come into contact with in the course of the narrative. As with *Verre cassé*, the local community bar is the focal point for the gathering of a number of very colourful and entertaining regulars, who regale us with the stories of their abject lives. These narratives do not, however, work simply as somewhat naïve sociological or 'ethnological' recordings, but are acutely self-aware and self-reflexive, all the while being narrated from the point of view of a subject that is 'less than human' or 'other than human'. These figures could indeed be described as *immonde*, that is, not so much 'abject' in terms of a psychologized Kristevan dynamic of expulsion and return of subjective otherness,[10] as 'un-worldly' in the sense in which Nancy describes it in *The Creation of the World*. While this term for Nancy is aligned with the 'bad infinity' of globalization which he critiques, for Mbembe, and the writers who take their cue from his theorization of postcolonial Africa, this becomes a kind of negative foundational moment, as Nganang has characterized it. So in the latter's *Temps de chien*, the dog-narrator, Mboudjak, gets brutally mistreated by his master, Massa Yo, and is then hanged and left for dead by his son, Soumi. Mboudjak somehow survives, frees himself, and returns to Massa Yo and his son, who react at first with terror, but who eventually (if still grudgingly) take him back. He spends much of the rest of the novel sitting in a corner in Massa Yo's bar, *Le Client est roi* (*The Customer is King*), a vantage-point from which he observes all the many daily conversations and goings-on. Like the porcupine in Mabanckou's novel *Mémoires de porc-épic*, the dog narrator, Mboudjak is constantly hovering on the borderline between life and death, appears to die, and then to live on after death.

In one episode a mysterious, taciturn figure called Corbeau (Crow) shows up at the bar, and in a typically playful *mise-en-abîme*, we learn that Corbeau is a writer who is writing a novel called *Temps de chien*, in which he aims to record the lives and conversations of the characters in the bar. Once the purpose of his visits is discovered, his very presence generates deep suspicion and mistrust, even though he is the only one to intervene during a police raid one day, and to protest the unwarranted arrest of one of the regulars, *L'ingénieur* (*The Engineer*). This is Mboudjak's very characteristic reflection on the mistreatment Corbeau receives from the regulars:

'We should get this owl out of the neighbourhood'.
These were the most dreadful words ever uttered about the writer of our miserable lives. And I suddenly realised, in a stake of shock, the treatment that the engineer, the very person who had escaped with his life by curling up and hiding away in my master's yard, would have given to me, who also spent all my time simply observing humans, if I had been human. Simply out of pure professional solidarity as a co-observer, I sympathized with the philosopher.[11]

Writing, and writers, are viewed with suspicion, even hostility by the local community, and Mboudjak the dog's identification with the abject and rejected figure of the writer positions him figuratively as a kind of post-genocidal narrator. By association and extension, Nganang's own literary practice works as a performative enactment which also occupies this space of 'post-human' philosophical (in the sense in which Nganang uses it) invention, or reinvention. This is precisely the space of the African subject that Mbembe gestures towards in *On the Postcolony*, and indeed has articulated more forcefully in *Sortir de la grande nuit*, where he refers to literature's power as being a 'lieu de provocation' (*SGN*, 225) (site of provocation), which is perhaps a synonymous term for 'dissident literature'. Indeed, such figures of dissidence or subversion traverse Mbembe's work, from his early texts on underground political resistance in South Cameroon, and his study of Christian conversion in Africa, *Afriques indociles*, which radically challenged received wisdom about its seamless complicity with the colonial mission, and theorized 'indocility' as a subversively creative re-appropriation of selected elements of Christianity.[12]

Much contemporary African literature, of which the novels of Nganang and Mabanckou serve as resonant examples in a Francophone context, could be said to be situated very much within the realm of the *immonde*, beginning with Mudimbe's 1973 novel of the story of a prostitute's love affair with a government minister in the urban underworld of Democratic Republic of Congo (formerly Zaire), *Le bel immonde*.[13] One could think of countless non-Francophone examples, from Yvonne Vera's *Nehanda* to J. M. Coetzee's *Disgrace*, to Chimamanda Adichie's *Half of a Yellow Sun*, itself an example of what might indeed be something of an entire sub-genre, the child-soldier novel. Literature, or what I am terming more broadly the 'literary', is thus both a privileged site for the expression of contemporary African abjection, where life and death dramas are played out in a tragic mode devoid of any grandeur, and at the same time the necessary negative moment through which the opening of 'dis-enclosure' becomes possible. As Mbembe reminds us in his foreword to the second French edition of *De la postcolonie*, this negativity is anything but the 'Afropessimism' of which he is often accused.[14]

A brief detour through Claire Denis's stark and disturbing vision of postcolonial Africa, her 2009 film *White Material*, illustrates how much broader a concept and process the 'literary' might be. Her film, taken at the level of its narrative alone, might simply be read as a political allegory of the continued colonial influence in Africa: Maria Vial as the white French coffee plantation owner, in the midst of a deepening civil war, refuses to 'let go' of her attachment to Africa, precisely because she considers herself as African as the native black Africans. The film, like much of Denis's work, operates at the same time on a far more disorienting, visceral, sensual level, not just in terms of its complex temporal narrative structure, but also through its foregrounding of strong textures, its haunting and disturbing images, and its dissonant soundtrack. What it presents, of course, is a profoundly disjunctive relationship between Africa and the West, but it goes much further in artistic terms, since it is ultimately concerned with a rupture between, on the one hand, received understandings of the meaning of 'Africa', and its reality on the other, a disjunction between economic logic (growing and trading coffee on the world market) and lived reality (the impossibility of succeeding economically, given both local and global conditions). In aesthetic terms, this becomes a more radical rupture between sense and the senses, and indeed, to return to Nancy, one might reframe this as a distinction between globalization and *mondialisation*. The senses in fact, according to Nancy, seem innately to resist any attempt to bring them under the control of sense, and this uncontrollable profusion, or what he has termed 'anarchic exuberance' of the senses, is such that philosophical systems which attempt to give order and meaning to this anarchy do so only at the cost of negating the extraordinary sensual richness which Nancy locates at the very origin and heart of sense-making.[15] Nancy's work provides a conceptual framework for rethinking how we might approach the question of the senses and sensuality in contemporary Africa, as it has been conventionally understood and historically determined, as well as the nature of the 'world', and what it might mean for Africa to talk of its 'own' world.

The Literary and the Global

At the heart of what I am terming broadly 'the literary' in contemporary Africa, then, are various figures or operations of rupture, dissonance or dissidence. At the most obvious thematic level, these could be said to represent the fragmented, even shattered subject of contemporary postcolonial Africa. If one takes such figures as symptomatic of a more deep-seated philosophical concern, and following Nganang's thesis about literature and the post-genocidal negative foundational moment, they reveal a necessary relationship of dissidence effecting an epistemological, even metaphysical break with a certain exhausted past and tradition. This entails a break with 'Africa' itself, or rather, with the manner in which it has hitherto represented itself. Mbembe has theorized this in terms of a break or rupture, a *faille* (*DP*, xxxii), and as a question of 'indocility', or *déclosion*, to borrow Nancy's term, and it can be aligned with Nancy's distinction between globalization and *mondialisation*. Indeed, this could well account for the turn that Mbembe and others have made recently towards the ideas of thinkers of difference, such as Derrida and Nancy, and the way in which they have theorized 'the literary'.

Literature, or at least a particular mode of dissident literature that takes its theoretical cue from Mbembe's analyses of postcolonial Africa, seems thus to have taken over from African philosophy, according to Nganang. It is no accident that Mbembe's own writing both describes in extensive and painful detail the 'life after death' of the African postcolony, but at the same time enacts it as a kind of spectral self-inscription within a history and a tradition. Mbembe's own ghostly, or spectral other is the figure of Ruben Um Nyobè, the Cameroonian political militant and journalist and founder of the nationalist, anti-colonial UPC, who was assassinated by the French in 1958, and who has been most famously commemorated by his compatriot Mongo Beti in his 1974 novel *Remember Ruben*, among others. Nganang is no doubt right to point to Mbembe as the most important commentator of the African postcolony, and one can now more readily understand Mbembe's influence on him. This can be seen in terms of the critical position he adopts with respect to the two broad traditions of African philosophy — indigenist and Marxist-inspired — but also his emphasis on a radically new subjective space that he is attempting to clear the way for. The 'worldliness' this implies — more Heideggerian in its ontological commitment — is perhaps a world away from the more assertive optimism of the *littérature-monde* manifesto. Nganang's characterization of 'post-genocide' literature is a controversial one, which has already been the subject of some fierce criticism, although its most significant gesture is perhaps in according literature — whether African, Francophone or global, however this is conceived — a far more central philosophical importance than it has traditionally been accorded. A number of questions remain, though, which I would like to explore briefly in conclusion, very much in the spirit of *déclosion*, hoping these might take us a few more steps along the paths that have been usefully opened up by Nganang.

I would suggest first of all, given the more all-embracing 'global' reach I am proposing for the 'literary', that while literature is privileged by Nganang and others as the site of a re-emergent philosophy, and specifically a philosophy of a differently conceived African subjectivity, I would suggest, along with Mbembe, that one ought to include other modes of cultural production (for example music, art, photography, film, sculpture, spirituality, and so on), whose artistic forms without doubt offer us equivalent creatively dissident practices in contemporary Africa.

Secondly, although both Mbembe and Nganang are proposing a new form of responsibility and autonomous agency for Africa, and more specifically a reinvented African subjectivity, within our contemporary 'global age', it would be important to reflect on what it would mean actively to 'write out' the relationship to the West, and Africa's colonial history. One might need to assess the long-term epistemological price to pay in taking 'the West' out of the equation of events like the Rwandan genocide (reading it as a will to autonomy that involves taking historical responsibility for the genocide, and in making this a story that has to do essentially with Africa's self-destruction, the failure and collapse of African philosophy). There is a risk, in other words, that the move away from a syndrome of victimization might inadvertently exculpate the West.

As a corollary to this, and given the emphasis Mbembe and Nganang place on the *writing* of a new dissident literature as the site of a 'post-genocide' African subjectivity, along with the re-emergence of a new mode of philosophizing within this literature of dissidence, it would seem that we may need a comparable (dissident?) *reading* practice. That is, if we are indeed dealing with a radically new form of being in the world (nothing can ever be the same post-genocide), then we can no longer read as we once did. It seems important to determine what such a dissident, or disjunctive, mode of reading would consist of. Just as writing, and the literary, are being considered here as extending beyond the borders of what we might think of as contemporary literature, this new reading practice would in effect gesture towards a whole new aesthetic sensibility, or receptivity.

This is, of course, as we noted early on, very different in mood and intention from the celebratory gesture and aspiration of the *littérature-monde* manifesto, and it is important not to lose sight of the more sober context of Nganang's thesis, or Mbembe's stark analysis of the violent imaginary of the African postcolony. Alongside his literary analysis and foregrounding of writers such as Mabanckou, Nganang in his own manifesto text returns insistently to the question of one woman survivor of the genocide as a constant refrain, and a question to those who failed to respond to the genocide (*'Where were you?'*). In this regard, as well as fictional texts, and characters who 'live on' after death, one would need to consider — quite distinctly, and with equal attention — the written and spoken testimony of actual survivors of the genocide, and the specific temporal and narrative complexities that inform such testimony. Indeed, the question 'How does one live on?', or survive, is of course far more than a philosophical question, or even the privileged question of philosophy as a new literary (or aesthetic) form, but it also has to do profoundly and fundamentally with questions of truth and reconciliation. How does one heal from such trauma? One cannot simply break with the past, especially not with a past as traumatic as a brutal genocide, and one might look here to the experience of the South African Truth and Reconciliation Commission, and the way in which it was able (more or less successfully) to separate out the question of amnesty — as the political and juridical social mechanism by which the transition is made from the apartheid era — from the moral (and psychological) dimension of forgiveness (that is, although political amnesty is granted with full disclosure of crimes, victims are not obliged to forgive or forget).[16]

One might finally consider the particular form and style of dissident literature proposed by Nganang from the perspective of gender, and whether we are still within the rather less-than-global realm of phallocracy, given that Mbembe's reading of the violent political imaginary in postcolonial Africa is explicitly masculinized, and given too that there is no escaping the fact that this is certainly the 'world' of the narratives of Sony Labou Tansi, Nganang and Mabanckou. Is this also ultimately another kind of phallogocentrism, and would this then become a *disabling* element in the claim to philosophical dissidence? In the previously mentioned foreword to the second French edition of *De la postcolonie*, Mbembe returns to this charge, which has been levelled most eloquently by Judith Butler in her insightful reading of an early version of Mbembe's 'Aesthetics of Vulgarity' chapter from *On the Postcolony*.[17] Mbembe, in his rejoinder to such criticisms, points out that he is attempting to describe the very clear phallic nature of the potentate's abusive exercise of power in postcolonial Africa, but that his theoretical intent is to foreground the sexualization of political power more broadly, and that while power is most often masculinized, his analysis covers a very wide and inclusive spectrum of sexual identities and sexual pleasures, both real and imaginary (*DP*, xxx).

We might then, of course, ask whether this pluralized sexual imaginary, in its inclusive relativism, undermines the singularly dissident force (the *im-monde* of globalization, so to speak) by which 'the literary' can stake out its counter-discursive claims. In other words, we might be led to conclude that Nganang's diagnosis of the current state, and prognosis of the future 'life after death', of African literature in French is ultimately one of many such examples of the polyphonic array which emerges out of the *littérature-monde* manifesto's breaking of the Francophone 'pact' with the nation, and it would thus appear to be entirely consistent with an approach to globalization which welcomes a heterogeneity of specific sites. I would argue, however, that what Nganang's text does, for all of the rather problematic implications around its edges, is to force us into a more sober, sustained, and philosophically serious engagement with each of the key terms in the *littérature-monde* debate — mostly notably the status of 'literature' and of the 'world', and the relation between the two in the context of contemporary Africa — and to make 'the literary' an unavoidable point of reference for any contemporary theory of globalization.

NOTES

1   That is, in the etymological sense of making or creating, *poiesis*, and just as Heidegger in his philosophy drew out the deep connection linking poetic language and thinking, *dichten* and *denken*, it is perhaps no accident that African literature, most notably Francophone, has its potent origin in poetic form. The importance of the publication of the celebrated *Anthologie de la nouvelle poésie nègre et malgache de langue française* in 1947, and Senghor's poetry more generally, has been rather occluded by the discredited essentialism of *Négritude* thought and writing. For an excellent account of the unacknowledged political power of Senghor's poetic imagination, see Gary Wilder, *The French Imperial Nation-State: Négritude and Colonial Humanism Between the Two World Wars* (Chicago: Chicago University Press, 2005).

2   Indeed, Mbembe himself has explicitly invoked and applied Nancy's ideas in his most recent text *Sortir de la Grande Nuit* (Paris: La Découverte, 2010); henceforward abbreviated with page numbers to *SGN*. For a more detailed analysis of Mbembe's complex 'debt' to both Nancy and Derrida, see Michael Syrotinski, 'Genealogical Misfortunes: Achille Mbembe's (Re-)Writing of Postcolonial Africa', *Paragraph* 35:3 (November 2012), 407–20.

3   *La création du monde, ou la mondialisation* (Paris: Galilée, 2002). Subsequent references, abbreviated to *CW* with page numbers, are to the English translation by François Raffoul and David Pettigrew, *The Creation of the World, or Globalization* (Albany, NY: SUNY Press, 2007).

4   Nancy, *The Inoperative Community*, edited by Peter Connor, translated by Peter Connor, Lisa Garbus, Michael Holland and Simona Sawhney, with a Foreword by Christopher Fynsk (Minneapolis: University of Minnesota Press, 1991).

5   Alain Mabanckou, *Verre Cassé* (Paris: Editions du Seuil, 2005), 11–12; *Broken Glass*, translated by Helen Stevenson (London: Serpent's Tail, 2009), 1–2. Subsequent references, abbreviated to *VC* with page numbers, are to this English translation.

6   *Pour une littérature-monde*, edited by Michel Le Bris and Jean Rouaud (Paris: Gallimard, 2007).

7   Patrice Nganang, *Manifeste d'une nouvelle littérature africaine: pour une écriture pré-emptive* (Paris: Editions Homnisphères, 2007). Henceforward abbreviated to *M*, followed by page numbers.

8   In my view, Nganang's dismissal of Mudimbe is rather harsh, and needs to be at the very least nuanced. Like Mbembe, Mudimbe is also critical of both indigenism (or what he would describe as the derivative nature of Africanist discourse, including its theologians like Mbiti, its linguists like Alexis Kagamé, its ethnophilosophers such as Placide Tempels, and its historians like Cheikh Anta Diop and Joseph Ki-Zerbo, as well as of the 'philosopher kings' of the early independence years, such as Nkrumah, Nyerere, Cabral and so on), and of Marxism, which he sees as yet one more version of a universalizing 'will to truth'. Mudimbe notes that the limits of Marxist-inspired political radicalism were clearly seen in the African countries that adopted Socialist programmes following Independence, and he states bluntly: 'African socialisms were a mystification and everyone knows it' (V. Y. Mudimbe, 'Anthropology and Marxist Discourse' in *Parables and Fables: Exegesis, Textuality and Politics in Central Africa* (Madison: University of Wisconsin Press, 1991), 183).

9   Achille Mbembe, *On the Postcolony* (Berkeley: University of California Press, 2001), 236.

10 See Julia Kristeva, *The Powers of Horror: An Essay on Abjection* (New York: Columbia University Press, 1982).

11 Patrice Nganang, *Temps de chien* (Paris: Le serpent à plumes, 2001), 157; my translation. English translation by Amy Reid, *Dog Days. An Animal Chronicle* (Charlottesville: University of Virginia Press, 2006).

12 Achille Mbembe, *Afriques indociles. Christianisme, pouvoir et état en société postcoloniale* (Paris: Editions Karthala, 1988).

13 V. Y. Mudimbe, *Le bel immonde* (Paris: Présence Africaine, 1976). English translation by Marjolijn de Jager, *Before the Birth of the Moon* (New York: Simon and Schuster, 1989). The English translation of the title bypasses the way in which the polarized tensions of the story are captured so evocatively by the French title.

14 As Mbembe puts it towards the end of this foreword, after responding to the various critiques to which the English edition, *On the Postcolony*, has been subjected: 'What we need to do, then, is to question life and the political in a different way, using categories whose heuristic value derives from their philosophical, literary, artistic, aesthetic and stylistic surplus value.

Ethnography, sociology, history or even political science have a role to play in this project. But this role is not a central one, and this is perhaps the price we have to pay to make Africa once more an enchanted place [*ré-enchanter l'Afrique*], and to bring it out of the ghetto in which "African studies" have imprisoned it' (Achille Mbembe, 'Avant-propos' in *De la postcolonie: Essai sur l'imagination politique dans l'Afrique contemporaine,* 2nd edition (Paris: Editions Karthala, 2012), xxxii). Future references to this work will be abbreviated to *DP*, followed by page references.

15 'Extraordinary Sense', Preface to Special Issue on 'Jean-Luc Nancy: Sense, The Senses, and The World', edited by Michael Syrotinski, *The Senses and Society* 8:3 (March 2013), 13.

16 For an insightful, philosophically informed discussion of this question, see Barbara Cassin, '"Removing the perpetuity of hatred": On South Africa as a Model Example', *International Review of the Red Cross* Vol. 88, No. 862 (June 2006), 235–44. For Cassin, the question of narrative truth is marked by an important shift away from a focus on disclosure as a 'revelation' of what was hidden, to a more finely tuned attentiveness to language as performative (reparative) act.

17 Judith Butler, 'Mbembe's Extravagant Power', *Public Culture* 5:1 (1992), 62–74.

The 'Unhomely' White Women of Antillean Writing

Maeve McCusker

Abstract:
While the field known as 'Whiteness Studies' has been thriving in Anglophone criticism and theory for over 25 years, it is almost unknown in France. This is partly due to epistemological and political differences, but also to demographic factors—in contrast with the post-plantation culture of the US, for example, whites in Martinique and Guadeloupe are a tiny minority of small island populations. Yet 'whiteness' remains a phantasized and a fetishized state in the Antillean imaginary, and is strongly inflected by gender. This article sketches the emergence of 'white' femininity during slavery, then examines its representation in the work of a number of major Antillean writers (Condé, Placoly, Confiant, Chamoiseau). In their work, a cluster of recurring images and leitmotifs convey the idealization or, more commonly, the pathologization, of the white woman; these images resonate strongly with Bhabha's 'unhomely', and convey the disturbing imbrication of sex and race in Antillean history.

Keywords: whiteness, *Békés*, Condé, Placoly, Confiant, Chamoiseau, Bhabha, unhomely

Introduction

In a 1998 essay on Shakespeare, Kim F. Hall declares that '[w]hiteness is enjoying a certain vogue, particularly in American Studies'. This vogue was, she argues, 'invigorated by Toni Morrison's call in *Playing in the Dark* to "discover, through a look at literary 'blackness', the nature — even the cause — of literary 'whiteness'"'.[1] Indeed over the last 25 years, an extraordinary wealth of publications, many of which use Morrison's essay as a springboard, testify to this 'vogue', from

Paragraph 37.2 (2014): 273–289
DOI: 10.3366/para.2014.0126
© Edinburgh University Press
www.euppublishing.com/para

Richard Dyer's classic study *White*,[2] through a raft of titles theorizing whiteness,[3] or exploring the representation of whiteness by a particular author.[4] Just as Masculinity Studies evolved as an outworking of, and a complement to, feminist criticism, so scholars of ethnicity and race, working in a range of fields from Psychoanalysis to Anthropology to Literary Studies, would as the 1990s progressed gravitate to another unexamined norm, whiteness. This norm, Ross Chambers argues, is in fact so prevalent in Western discourse that it should be seen not as a classificatory identity, but rather as synonymous with being human. Chambers continues, 'there are plenty of unmarked categories (maleness, heterosexuality, and middleclassness being obvious ones), but whiteness is perhaps the primary unmarked and so unexamined — let's say "blank" — category'.[5] In turn a chorus of critical voices, starting from the position that 'whiteness' is based on no epidermal or biological reality, would emphasize the slipperiness of 'race', its scientific invalidity, and its constructed or imagined status: a view attested in numerous titles (for example *Performing Whiteness*, *The Habit of Whiteness*),[6] and pithily summarized in Gerry Turcote's observation that the very idea of 'an isolated and pure whiteness' has always been 'a pigment of the white imagination'.[7] This de-essentializing of whiteness is an important first principle. The constructed nature of racial phenotypes should be taken as axiomatic for the present analysis, which is concerned with the *representation* of whiteness, and more particularly of white women, in recent Antillean literature.

Critics and theorists of Francophone post-slavery cultures, relative to their North American and British counterparts, have appeared to neglect whiteness as a structuring motif in culture and society. To give but one (admittedly crude) example, the search item 'whiteness' in the British Library catalogue produces 2395 results, while its ostensible equivalent, 'blancheur', gives only 65 notices in the Bibliothèque nationale de France,[8] none of which (excepting three editions of the French translation of *Playing in the Dark*), deal with whiteness as an ethnic classification. Indeed 'blancheur', although it is used by Morrison's translator for the essay's subtitle ('Blancheur et imagination littéraire'),[9] sounds an imperfect match for the signifier 'whiteness', while non-standard lexemes such as 'blanchitude' or 'békétude'[10] do not register in the catalogue at all. This apparent neglect of whiteness can be explained, on the one hand, in epistemological terms: the current vogue might be considered part of an 'Anglosaxon' Cultural Studies agenda, to which the French academy has been notoriously resistant.[11] Moreover, theoretical movements emanating from the

Antilles themselves initially privileged the other pole of the colour spectrum (*Négritude*) and, more recently, celebrated racial and cultural mixing (*Créolité*). Most importantly, though, there are good empirical reasons why the starting premiss of whiteness studies—the ubiquity and consequent 'invisibility' of whiteness, or as Chambers puts it, its status as a 'blank' category—is not especially illuminating in the Antilles. If white privilege in the West, as Shannon Sullivan argues, is 'unseen, invisible, even seemingly non-existent', and therefore operates as a 'set of unconscious psychical and somatic habits',[12] it could be argued that Martinique and Guadeloupe challenge, and in many respects invert, this paradigm. These islands' white communities have always been a tiny, self-segregating minority of already small populations.[13] As the subtitle of a rare monograph devoted to the caste indicates, Antillean whites are a 'dominant minority'.[14] This paradoxical status has distanced them from what we might call the 'banality' of racial privilege, or from the naturalization of whiteness as an unmarked category. Rather, the descendants of the white plantation-owning caste—known as *békés* in Martinique and *zoreys* in Guadeloupe[15]—experience if anything a heightened visibility, and an amplified sense of racial identity. Today, this keen awareness of ethnicity (their own and that of others) operates within a broader French Republican context which claims to be colour-blind, but in which whiteness is the inescapable, if unspoken, norm. These factors complicate(d) the position of white planters who, overwhelmingly outnumbered by their non-white neighbours throughout history, were always acutely aware of the fragility of their tenure and of their minority status. Their desire to maintain racial purity (*préserver la race*)[16] was to become a historical and socio-cultural counterweight to the impulse among non-whites, famously analysed by Fanon, to 'whiten' or 'save' the race,[17] or, in more colloquial terms, to *chaper la peau* (literally, to save or to escape one's skin): that is, to marry partners of a lighter skin tone, and thereby facilitate social ascension.

Given their minority demographic status, it is unsurprising that white characters have also been diegetically marginal in literature. Whiteness could be said to figure primarily as an absence in much twentieth-century writing, or perhaps more accurately, as a powerful absent-present. Often the *béké* master is literally an absentee, as in Joseph Zobel's *La Rue Cases-Nègres* (1950), or has been excluded from the narrative—responsible for primal crimes of rape that have led to the conception of fictional characters, but long-disappeared. At times he has been wilfully, indeed almost superstitiously, sidelined. In

Patrick Chamoiseau's *Texaco*, Esternome refuses to describe the *béké* to his daughter, 'fearing he would come back to haunt his old age'.[18] The same author's *L'Esclave vieil homme et le molosse* focuses on the intersubjective dynamic between master, slave and dog; yet its title names the old slave and the master's dog, but not the *béké*. And, if the *colon* is a marginal or repressed figure, the white woman could be said to be doubly invisible in contemporary literature. If she figures at all, she tends to be a shadowy, ephemeral, spectral or unreal presence, excessively idealized or, more frequently, pathologized: maimed, mute, blind or mad.

This essay offers, first, a brief historical contextualization of the emergence of 'white' femininity in the Antilles, and then examines its representation by four major Antillean writers (Maryse Condé, Vincent Placoly, Raphaël Confiant, Patrick Chamoiseau). The *béké* wife or daughter, although peripheral, is represented in the works examined here through a cluster of images and leitmotifs which, whether conveying her idealization or her pathologization, are strongly, and disturbingly, connected to the imbrication of sex and race in Caribbean society. On the one hand, as we will see in Condé's *Le Cœur à rire et à pleurer* (1999), the white woman projects impossible piety and chastity, qualities historically embedded in her position as guardian of racial 'purity' on the plantation. Much more commonly, however (and this is the case for all the other texts discussed here: Placoly's *Frères volcans* (1983); Condé's *Traversée de la Mangrove* (1989); Confiant's *Eau de café* (1991); and Chamoiseau's *L'Esclave vieil homme et le molosse* (1997) and *Un dimanche au cachot* (2007)), white women, in their alienation from the plantation, are presented as profoundly unhomely creatures. Homi Bhabha, drawing on Freud's theory of the *unheimlich*, the 'uncanny',[19] defines the unhomely as a 'paradigmatic colonial and postcolonial condition', in which 'the recesses of the domestic space become sites for history's most intricate invasions'.[20] Women are especially susceptible to the unhomely condition, in which 'the borders between home and world become confused', so that 'private and public, past and present, the psyche and the social develop an interstitial intimacy. It is an *intimacy that questions binary divisions*' (*Location*, 13, my emphasis). In the examples considered below, the home (known on the plantation as the *grand'case*), is repeatedly breached by the public sphere. This invasion takes the form of explicit political threat (the entry of abolitionist Victor Schœlcher into the planter's home in Chamoiseau's *Dimanche*; the 1848 revolution in Placoly's *Frères*), but also, at the familial level, is manifest in historically overdetermined sexual relationships which threaten the 'black and white' binary divisions on which slavery depends (interracial sex in *Traversée*; *béké* reproduction with a *négresse*, and sexual assault, in *Eau de café*; the shadow of incest in *L'Esclave vieil homme*). In these 'houses of racial memory' (*Location*, 9), something troubles the boundary between home and world, something which affects women first and most intimately, but which will have consequences beyond the private world of the home.

Whiteness Idealized

As Rebecca Hartkopf Schloss has shown, from the very earliest days of the plantation, colonists invested in the myth that they had come from 'good stock'. In a concerted effort to construct the plantation as an idealized order, and to delimit the boundaries of whiteness, they 'crafted an ideal of white masculinity', according to which white men were 'loving fathers and faithful spouses within stable white households'. Meanwhile white women were cast 'as the physical guardians of white purity and as custodians of the cultural markers of white identity'. As Schloss argues, '[i]n practice this meant that white women should have only marital sex and then only with white men. It also required that white women eschew work in favour of a life of relative financial ease, focused on mothering'. White women were crucial to the perpetuation of *béké* wealth, because children inherited the status of their mothers. Those who bore children out of wedlock to non-white men 'presented a significant threat to white hegemony by contributing to the growth of [the] *gens de couleur*'.[21] A strong correlation therefore developed in plantation society between motherhood and lightness of skin, itself understood to be a marker of saintliness and religious deity. In this coercive regime, women were constructed as idealized mothers or virginal angels, both archetypes designed to keep hybridity at bay.

Maryse Condé's childhood memoir, *Le Cœur à rire et à pleurer*,[22] explores this idealized projection of female whiteness. Condé insists on the racial stratification of Guadeloupe. Only two white characters are encountered on the island; the first may well be a figment of the narrator's imagination (or subconscious),[23] the second is worshipped from afar. In a *locus classicus* of black writing, to be found in the work of Zobel, Morrison, Mayotte Capécia and many others, the narrator, in church, observes the iconography of Christianity — the statues of

St Anthony of Padua, Thérèse of Lisieux, Michael the Archangel, the baby Jesus — in all of its bleached piety. Noting the scarcity of 'black or even coloured faces'[24] in the cathedral's central aisle — ostensibly reserved for the town's bourgeoisie — she concludes that the few non-white faces in these elite ranks stand out as though they had, in their attempt to assimilate, fallen into the bowl of milk of the famous nursery rhyme:

A black woman was drinking milk/ Ah, she said to herself, if only I could/ Dip my face in a bowl of milk/ I'd become whiter/Than all the French/ Ah-Ah-Ah!

The central aisle is a space in which white power, usually invisibly present in the Antilles, is made visible; the assigned pews group whites together in a rare vision of communion and community, while black worshippers are mostly relegated to inferior seats. Sunday mass therefore offers the narrator — trained to avoid the gaze of even her white classmates outside school — a rare opportunity to scrutinize the white face. A cluster of verbs of motion — 'my gaze climbed, descended, scoured the rows of faces' — registers excitement and scopophilia, although the look is more of bemusement and curiosity ('my slightly mocking exploration') than of awe. The faces she sees are characterized by arched noses and thin lips, and are 'marked by the same seal of yellowish paleness'.

   The narrator's gaze then falls upon a young woman, 'a black straw hat planted on her tawny hair, her forehead half covered by a veil, her velvety cheeks, her rosebud lips. She was wearing a beige linen suit, a cameo brooch pinned on the lapel'. What attracts her are precisely the markings of heightened whiteness which set the woman apart from the red earlobes and the yellowish tones of the supposedly white congregation. She emerges from this encroaching redness and yellowness, the black hat offsetting her whiteness through contrast, the pink of her rosebud lips mirroring those of the statue of Thérèse, her attire the classic vestments of the *colon* caste (pale linen and, the following Sunday, white lace). Her 'whiter than white' appeal is conveyed through repeated superlatives: the chapter is entitled 'The most beautiful woman in the world'; the narrator states that she had 'never seen anything so perfect', and that the woman has 'an inimitable grace'. In the sanctioned and sanctified space of the church, the white imago would appear to ward off the errant forces of sexual desire, and therefore any hint of racial transgression — a transgression latent in the references to her fellow *zoreys* with their red earlobes and their yellowing skin. This sense of crafted perfection is mirrored in her cameo brooch which, like the statue of Thérèse, is what we might call an *objet en abyme*, featuring an idealized white face.

The child's first encounter with the mesmerizing power, and compelling otherness, of whiteness, culminates in her declaration that the woman is her 'ideal of beauty'. However, confronted with the disapproval of her mother and her beloved brother, she denies that it is the woman's whiteness that she admires. Yet she acknowledges, too, that the woman's pink skin, pale eyes and cascading hair are intrinsic to her beauty, conveying by implication that the values of white society have been internalized. It is a moment of classic disavowal, an 'ambivalent ego defence' in which, as Celia Britton has shown with reference to Fanon, 'the subject both recognizes and refuses to recognize an unwelcome perception'.[25]

What is of particular interest here is the juxtaposition of this scene with the remembered rhyme, quoted above, in which a black woman fantasizes about being whiter than white, whiter indeed than it is humanly possible to be. Milk, of course, is a classic symbol of whiteness; ingestion of, or immersion in, milk, is often figured in terms of an imagined metamorphosis or transubstantiation, a performative whiting up which gives its name to what Frantz Fanon, in *Black Skin, White Masks* (a text continually invoked in Condé's memoir), describes as the desire for 'lactification'.[26] But the rhyme has relevance not only for the black spectator, enthralled by white beauty, but also, perhaps especially, for the white subject herself. What Fanon, drawing on Gabriel Marcel, has described as 'the dialectic of being and having' (*Black Skin*, 44) with regards to whiteness is also subtly suggested in the portrait of the white woman. With reference to Fanon's dialectic, Valérie Loichot has shown how, in the presentation of his plantation-owner father, Saint-John Perse insists on 'possessions, on peripheral attributes', thereby suggesting 'a lack of being and authority'.[27] Loichot invokes Fanon's 'confusion between being and having', showing how objects and disembodied body parts are used to authenticate whiteness in a context of suspected 'contamination' (the father's mule-coloured skin is emphasized by the poet). In many ways Condé's description of the white imago depends equally on association, peripheral attributes and contrast; the woman's whiteness is accentuated by *association* with the statues that surround her, by *contrast* with her fellow *zoreys*, and by her *ownership* of talismans and emblems: white lace; her cameo brooch. She too embodies white anxieties around whiteness, and the fact that 'one has whiteness rather than is white' (*Orphan Narratives*, 107). Indeed the woman's name, Linsseuil, composed as it is of the words for linen and threshold, itself points to liminality, suggesting ambiguity rather than security of identity.

The narrator fails to engage the gaze of the woman: 'Suddenly her eyes met mine and, to my great pain, they turned away immediately, containing only indifference'. The following Sunday, glimpsing the *békée* coming into church, the child does not turn to look at her. The normative scopic regime has been re-established, and the chapter concludes with the line 'I'd understood that her beauty was forbidden to me'.

Whiteness Pathologized

Condé's memoir explores an admiring, pre-pubescent female gaze on female whiteness, in the sanctioned public space of the cathedral, and thus tends towards a knowingly naive idealization of the white woman (even while suggesting the possibility of her contamination). Other texts privilege the more intimate domestic context of the *grand'case*, and work to pathologize rather than to idealize white femininity. In these works white women are generally seen not in communitarian terms but rather as isolated, alienated, intensely lonely and usually house-bound individuals.

Condé's 1989 novel *Traversée de la mangrove* exemplifies and undermines these tropes, notably in the extent to which characters embodying what we might call 'structural' whiteness are in fact of mixed race.[28] The landowning patriarch Loulou Lameaulnes celebrates the white 'discoverers' in his lineage (127), and identifies most closely with his *béké* ancestor Gabriel, who had been rejected by his family for marrying a black woman (103). Loulou fashions himself, quite literally, as a *béké*: he wears the panama hat and the white suit of the *colon* (123; 102), lives far from the locals, behind 'arrogant railings', employs servants and 'lords it up' (22), while dreaming of supplying flowers to the Queen of England (121). His first wife, Aurore, dies at the age of thirty from a fibroid, a tumour of the womb, suggesting the reproductive difficulties of the *béké* family and by extension of the caste. She is described as being 'si blême, si blême, qu'on savait qu'elle était en sursis sur cette terre' (53) (so wan, so wan, that people knew she wasn't long for this earth). The signifier *blême*— defined in *Le Petit Robert* as a 'blancheur maladive', an unhealthy whiteness, and which derives from an old Scandinavian word for blue, therefore connoting death[29] — is in fact commonly used to describe Creole women in literature. Loulou, one of the most brutish individuals in a text peopled by unsympathetic characters, dismisses her as 'a completely useless [*inutilisable*] wife' (124). Dinah, Loulou's second wife, comes from Saint-Martin and is half Dutch, half Indonesian. Yet her structural function in the novel and in the community — and notably the fact that she has no 'slave' blood — is very much that of the classic *békée* wife. She begins her married life with gusto, attempting, significantly, to disinfect the house. Her stepdaughter, Mira, recalls how she opened the windows wide, and scrubbed the house from top to bottom (53). But Dinah, too, rapidly declines in the space of the home. She is forbidden by Loulou to work in the family business, on the basis that '[t]he Lameaulnes women have always had enough to occupy them at home' (103). Isolated, and humiliated by her husband's infidelity, Dinah describes the home as a prison and a tomb, and declares that as the years unfurled 'I felt like I was already dead, that my blood ran cold in my veins, that it was already curdled' (103–4). This living death — Mira describes her as a 'zombie' (57) — is specifically linked to her husband's sexual disinterest. Dinah retreats to a locked bedroom every evening, curling up in the foetal position, while Loulou leaves the home to spend the night with a variety of other women.

Traversée is a novel by a female writer who has always been attentive to the position of women; it puts women's experience at its core, famously privileges a range of female narrative voices, and examines a broad cross-section of Guadeloupean society. What is interesting, however, is the extent to which the association of white femininity — never a *central* axis of interest in any of the texts under discussion — with torpor, stasis, confinement, illness and incapacity, emerges in a fairly codified manner as a common leitmotif in work by male authors too.

Vincent Placoly's *Frères volcans*,[30] alone in our corpus, puts *béké* characters centre-stage. It is an unusual example of a 'black' writer deploying a sole 'white' narrator. Set in Martinique during the turmoil of 1848, the story is told from the perspective of an enlightened *béké* confined to bed because of old age and illness. The narrator configures life in the Antilles as a form of mental and physical degeneration for whites of both sexes, commenting that 'Blacks can see things we can't (...) they live closer to life than us' (22). This inability to see, and consequent lack of vitality, is especially true for women, who 'are more dead than alive', and for whom '[t]his slow death can be read on their faces, and especially in their gazes, which they run over all things without seeing them' (40). Their living death, manifest in a vacant stare, is first and foremost a form of intellectual disengagement: confined to the home or the convent, women withdraw from history and politics in favour of fiction and romance:

> Disciplined in the convent, following in all activities the book of society, convinced by religion that their time on earth lasts only as long as God wills, [the white woman] has only the vaguest idea of history. The books she reads in the shadow of the veranda contain no history; they are romantic novels. (40)

The veranda, a classic liminal zone between the private and the public, is where reading, with its connexion to the outside world, conventionally takes place. But the threat of the world is ostensibly (and self-defensively?) neutralized by women's preference for fiction over history, allowing, presumably, a withdrawal from political realities.

The narrator had considered marriage to a planter's daughter, Vive Laguerre — an ironic name given the associations of white femininity with indolence, death and passivity. Vive is a pleasant but frivolous gossip, who 'can't see the deeper meaning of things' (42). Indeed in one of the most poignant moments of the novel Vive herself acknowledges the living death of the plantation:

> Nous sommes condamnés [*sic*] à rêver le huis clos de la liberté. Vous savez bien que toutes les femmes ici languissent après les chimères voraces de leur sang et de leur vitalité. C'est pourquoi nous sommes alourdies de silence, puisque les illusions n'ont pas de voix. (43)

> (We are condemned to dream about the closed doors of freedom. You know that all women here languish after the insatiable whims of their blood and vitality. That's why we're weighed down by silence, since illusions have no voice.)

The reference to 'insatiable whims' reinforces a stereotype of the Creole woman as decadent and sexually lascivious; but Vive's description of the female condition through terms such as 'chimeras', 'dream', 'illusions' also connotes fantasy, and a withdrawal into the world of the supernatural. The living death of white women derives from their frustrated sexual desire, given that the whims of their 'blood' and 'vitality' are repressed. A later comment by the narrator confirms the sexual dysfunction of the plantation: 'We Creoles (. . .) have deserted our women's wombs' (62). The plantation has become a sterile space of stifled sexuality, in which renewal and regeneration (within the caste at least) are no longer possible.

In Raphaël Confiant's *Eau de café*,[31] too, white women are presented in terms of withdrawal, invisibility and madness. Whether the wives of local policemen, or the spouse and daughter of the *béké* Honoré de Cassagnac,[32] they never venture outside the home (23; 231); Cassagnac's daughter Marie-Eugénie is so reclusive that she is not seen even at church (36). Conscious of the lack of renewal in his family's genes, Cassagnac had sought a wife in Anjou rather than in Martinique. Like Dinah in *Traversée*, his bride initially appears to thrive in the plantation house, giving birth to a daughter and to two sons; and like Dinah, her decline is linked to the sexual disinterest of her husband. When Cassagnac begins to sleep with a *négresse*, Franciane, she 'wilts' (the verb 's'étioler', a botanical term meaning to bleach through the exclusion of sunlight, reinforces the connexion between whiteness and decline). Her speech becomes barely audible, she falls into a 'frightening indifference', and becomes 'lost in a *chimera*' (321, my emphasis — the signifier also used by Placoly to describe Vive's uncanny trance-like state). When Franciane becomes pregnant, Cassagnac's wife definitively descends into madness ('déraison'), becoming so pale that her veins are visible through her skin. Here again whiteness is associated with sickness and decay. Marie-Eugénie, the *béké*'s daughter, later suffers a mysterious sexual assault in her father's house during carnival, which leaves her 'blinded by stupor' and incapable of speech or laughter (43): 'Her movements were jerky, almost mechanical. You'd have sworn she was one of those strange dolls with a mechanism in their back allowing them to talk or to raise an arm' (38). Bhabha reminds us of Freud's association of the uncanny with dolls and automata (*Location*, 136), figures whose eeriness derives from their indeterminacy, in particular their straddling of life and death.

The decline of mother and daughter is linked to the history of sexuality in plantation society, and to the confusion of 'home' and 'world'. In the case of the former, the planter's preference for sex with his black slave (known in Creole as the *femme dewo* — 'femme dehors', outside woman — the local term reasserting the mistress's position outside the home) over the legitimate spouse re-enacts the behaviour of white masters through history. In the case of the latter, the sexual assault is carried out *in the béké's home* by Julien Thémistocle, descendent of maroon slaves, and the historic enemy of the slave-owning caste. In both cases, it is an 'intimacy that questions binary divisions' (*Location*, 13), causing madness in the women affected and signalling the inevitable decline of the *béké* family and, by extension, the plantocracy.

Chamoiseau's 1997 novel, *L'Esclave vieil homme et le molosse*,[33] set in the 1830s, similarly foregrounds stasis, degeneration and lack of renewal. The plantation is already an anachronism; its machines date from the time of Père Labat, and the master is a 'conquistador fallen from a fold of time'. But women suffer the burden of plantation life most intimately. The *béké*'s daughter 'blinks her eyelids on too-fixed pupils', while his wife's 'voiceless melancholy' is occasionally interrupted by 'an old dramatic laugh' (19–21). Women are thus associated with the vacuous gaze, passive silence and hysteria. A later novel, *Un Dimanche au cachot*,[34] picks up these same anonymous characters, describing a 'maître et sa très-blanche' (106) (a master and his very-white) — the racial adjective has become a noun, and the white woman, also described as 'blême' (62), has been reduced to a racial type devoid of subjectivity and individuality. In a sinister moment, the *béké*

flatte de la main le blond de ses enfants, leurs tignasses flavescentes dont il a calculé l'émergence, la pâleur de sa femme choisie de juste blancheur: un cercle de pureté dans cette mangrove qui infecte l'humain... (65).

(caresses his children's blondness, their yellowing mops whose emergence he'd thought out so carefully, the paleness of a wife chosen uniquely for her whiteness: a circle of purity in this humanity-contaminating mangrove)

Once more in the slippage from adjective to noun, 'le blond', the colour of hair becomes reified, a thing to be engineered and cultivated. But the lack of genetic renewal feared by Cassagnac in Confiant's *Eau de café* is here starkly configured. This apparent 'circle of purity' is in fact a defensive and hermetically closed community, capable neither of freeing any of its members, nor of admitting others. If the *béké*'s wife was chosen solely for her whiteness, the children are described as 'flavescents', turning yellow, a symptom of decadence and degeneration, and the scene graphically demonstrates how the *béké*'s dread of hybridity has made a dead end of the plantation. Incest is obliquely suggested, as the father caresses children turned in upon themselves, defensively poised to repel the other, and therefore to neutralize the threat of that other taboo, miscegenation. Readers familiar with Chamoiseau's work will recognize the irony in the reference to the mangrove which, with its energy, multiplicity and organic cross-fertilization is a favoured metaphor for the chaotic intermingling of Creole society; this healthy, sustainable organism is a clear foil to the stagnation of the white family circle. Crucially, the family is host to an unnamed visitor, a porcelain seller, newly arrived from Alsace, whose enlightened views on abolition pose a direct threat to the plantocracy. The reader recognizes the intruder to be Victor Schœlcher, the leading French abolitionist (though Chamoiseau stresses Schœlcher's 'gradualist' perspective in terms of emancipation). Once more the recesses of the private space are being penetrated by political change, and the threat to the organism comes from both within and without.

Conclusion

The marginality of white characters in recent cultural production in the Antilles, in addition to the factors sketched above, may reflect a broader societal perception; Edouard Glissant suggests that '*Békés* were never seen by the mass of slaves, who then became agricultural workers, as *the real enemy*'.[35] Glissant argues that the invisible forces of globalization — instigated and controlled by metropolitan France — are the true enemy of the Antillean. And yet whiteness, as embodied in the *béké* ethnocaste, remains at once an aspiration and a repugnant reminder of the slave past, a phantasized and fetishized state. One need look no further than the strikes of 2009, or the fallout from the documentary of the same year, *Les Derniers Maîtres de la Martinique*,[36] to see that whiteness continues to command much more than cultural or imaginary capital in the French Antilles.

   In terms of the gender politics of the plantation, the pre-eminent position of the white patriarch undoubtedly served to marginalize *all* women, whites included. Hilary McD. Beckles's 'White Women and Slavery in the Caribbean', while dealing primarily with the Anglophone islands, is relevant here. Beckles commends recent work by Barbara Bush that has, without underplaying the privileged position of white women under slavery, also highlighted 'the common ground where womanhood in general was the target and prey of white male patriarchal authority'.[37] Although some recent novels explore the fragility and vulnerability of the master, white women characters are repeatedly shown to be victims of white male neglect and brutality. In terms of the small but representative corpus that has been examined here, fiction would seem to bear out, or indeed to prefigure, historiography. The suffering of the white woman and her detachment or exclusion from history and ideology are established literary tropes. This detachment, rightly or wrongly, conforms to historiographical research; Beckles contrasts the historiography of the Southern US states, which often positions women as the 'conscience' of the regime, with recent Caribbean historiography which asserts, perhaps erroneously, Beckles suggests, white women's 'relative unimportance to ideological formation within the history of the colonial complex' (67).

At the fictional level, it is precisely when history penetrates 'the recesses of the domestic space', to return to Bhabha's formulation (and in French the term *habitation* ironically emphasizes dwelling and a sense of being 'chez soi'), that the unhomeliness and dis-ease of white femininity emerges. Whether it be in the guise of historically overdetermined sexual relationships between white patriarch and black woman (Condé and Confiant), or in the form of perverted sexuality (rape or incest in Condé and Chamoiseau), or in the more worldly form of explicit political threat (the stirrings of revolution and abolition — Placoly and Chamoiseau), women come to experience what Bhabha, quoting Henry James, calls 'the house of darkness, the house of dumbness, the house of suffocation' (*Location*, 10). In these unhomely sites, sexuality and reproduction are radically and multiply disturbed: Condé's Dinah, in *Traversée*, coiled up nightly in the foetal position while her husband seeks pleasure with black women, or Loulou's young bride dead from a fibroid at thirty; Placoly's abandoned wombs; Confiant's traumatized doll-like daughter, violated by a maroon and rendered mute and blind; Chamoiseau's silent 'très-blanche', chosen uniquely for her whiteness. In these novels, whiteness comes to signify disease and degeneration, communication becomes displaced by voicelessness, the vacant stare and madness, and the unhomely becomes synonymous with the white female condition.

NOTES

1   Kim F. Hall, '"These Bastard Signs of Fair": Literary whiteness in Shakespeare's sonnets' in *Postcolonial Shakespeares*, edited by Ania Loomba and Martin Orkin (London and New York: Routledge, 1998), 64–83 (64).

2   Richard Dyer, *White* (London and New York: Routledge, 1997).

3   It would be impossible to give any representative sense of the range of titles and approaches involved. In addition to those quoted in this article, the studies I have found most useful include: Kalpana Seshadri-Crooks, *Desiring Whiteness. A Lacanian Analysis of Race* (London and New York: Routledge, 2000); *Displacing Whiteness. Essays in Social and Cultural Criticism*, edited by Ruth Frankenburg (Durham, NC: Duke University Press, 1999).

4   Two notable examples are Lucia Villares, *Examining Whiteness. Reading Clarice Lispector Through Bessie Head and Toni Morrison* (Oxford: Legenda, 2011) and

Faulkner and Whiteness, edited by Jay Watson (Jackson, MS: University Press of Mississippi, 2011).

5 Ross Chambers, 'The Unexamined' in *Whiteness. A Critical Reader*, edited by Mike Hill (New York: New York University Press, 1997), 187–203 (189).

6 Gwendolyn Audrey Foster, *Performing Whiteness. Postmodern Re/Constructions in the Cinema* (Albany, NY: State University of New York Press, 2003); Terrance McMullan, *Habits of Whiteness. A Pragmatist Reconstruction* (Bloomington: Indiana University Press, 2009).

7 Gerry Turcote, 'Vampiric Decolonization. Fanon, "Terrorism" and Mudrooroo's Vampire Trilogy' in *Postcolonial Whiteness: A Critical Reader on Race and Empire*, edited by Alfred J. Lopenz (Albany, NY: State University of New York Press, 2005), 103–118 (110).

8 Even its English equivalent, *whiteness*, gives 99 hits in the in the BNF catalogue. These figures are correct as of August 2013.

9 *Jouer dans le noir. Blancheur et imagination littéraire*, translated by Pierre Alien (Paris: Christian Bourgois, 1992).

10 This term has limited currency, but is a preferable alternative to 'blancheur', naming as it does an ethnocaste rather than a race.

11 Anne Chalard-Filladeau, 'From Cultural Studies to Etudes culturelles, Etudes de la culture, and Sciences de la culture in France. Questions of Singularity', *Cultural Studies* 23:5–6 (2009), 831–54, is a useful analysis of the epistemological reasons underpinning this resistance.

12 Shannon Sullivan, *Revealing Whiteness. The Unconscious Habits of Racial Privilege* (Bloomington, IN: Indiana University Press, 2006), 1.

13 Recent estimates—including in Romain Bolzinger's 2009 documentary *Les Derniers Maîtres de la Martinique* (Canal Plus, first broadcast 6 February 2009)—put their number at 1% of the Martinican population.

14 See Edith Kovátz-Beaudoux's *Les Blancs Créoles de la Martinique. Une minorité dominante* (Paris: L'Harmattan, 2002).

15 The origins of both these terms are contested. For *béké*, see Raphaël Confiant, http://kapeskreyol.potomitan.info/dissertation1d.html#4, consulted 2 August 2013, 6pm. For *zorey*, a term also used in the Indian Ocean, see Robert Chaudenson, *Lexique du parler créole de La Réunion* (Paris: Champion, 1974).

16 The term is still current, and is used for example by the *béké* Alain Huygues-Despointes in *Les Derniers Maîtres de la Martinique*.

17 Frantz Fanon, *Black Skin, White Masks*, translated by Charles Lam Markmann (New York: Grove Press, 1967), 47.

18 Patrick Chamoiseau, *Texaco*, translated by Rose-Myriam Réjouis and Val Vinokurov (London: Granta, 1997), 47.

19 Space does not permit a fuller discussion of Freud's uncanny. For a brilliant discussion of Bhabha's selective use of Freud, and his theory of the Unhomely

generally, see Celia M. Britton, 'Delirious Language. Living in the Unhomely World', Chapter 5 of *Edouard Glissant and Postcolonial Theory. Strategies of Language and Resistance* (Charlottesville and London: University Press of Virginia, 1999), 119–36.

20 Homi Bhabha, *The Location of Culture* (London and New York: Routledge, 1994), 9.

21 Rebecca Hartkopf Schloss, *Sweet Liberty. The Final Days of Slavery in Martinique* (Philadelphia: University of Pennsylvania Press, 2009), 6–7. Hilary McD. Beckles argues that white women procreating with slaves 'was not as uncommon as generally suggested' ('White Women and Slavery in the Caribbean', *History Workshop* 36 (1993), 66–82 (69)).

22 Maryse Condé, *Le Cœur à rire et à pleurer. Contes vrais de mon enfance* (Paris: Robert Laffont, 1999). All translations are mine, unless indicated otherwise.

23 In the first encounter a white girl physically abuses the narrator, explaining herself in terms of racial history: 'I have to hit you because you're black'. The adult narrator wonders whether this was in fact a supernatural encounter, an acting out of the unfinished traumas of slavery, and whether they were simply 'the reincarnation of a mistress and her punch-bag' (44).

24 All subsequent quotations from *Le Cœur* are from the chapter 'La plus belle femme du monde', 73–9.

25 Celia Britton, *Race and the Unconscious. Freudianism in French Caribbean Thought* (Oxford: Legenda, 2002), 40.

26 Fanon, *Black Skin*, 47.

27 Valérie Loichot, *Orphan Narratives. The Postplantation Literature of Faulkner, Glissant, Morrison, and Saint-John Perse* (Charlottesville and London: University of Virginia Press, 2007), 107.

28 Maryse Condé, *Traversée de la mangrove* (Paris: Folio, 1989).

29 See for example the *Dictionnaire culturel de la langue française*, edited by Alain Rey (Paris: Robert, 2005): 'Blêmir: issu du francique *blesmjan (...) l'ancien norrois blàmi désignant une couleur sombre, bleue', 956. See too the *Dictionnaire de la langue française*, edited by Emile Littré (Paris: Hachette, 1885): 'D'après Diez, de l'ancien scandinave, blâmi, couleur bleue, de blâ, bleu', I, 358.

30 Vincent Placoly, *Frères volcans. Chronique de l'abolition de l'esclavage* (Paris: La Brèche, 1983).

31 Raphaël Confiant, *Eau de Café* (Paris: Grasset & Fasquelle, 1991), 23.

32 The family shares the name of one of the most vociferous pro-slavery writers of the nineteenth century, Granier de Cassagnac.

33 Patrick Chamoiseau, *L'Esclave vieil homme et le molosse* (Paris: Gallimard, 1997).

34 Patrick Chamoiseau, *Un dimanche au cachot* (Paris: Gallimard, 2007).

35 Edouard Glissant, *Caribbean Discourse. Selected Essays*, translated with an introduction by J. Michael Dash (Charlottesville: University Press of Virginia, 1989), 39, emphasis in original.

36 See for example *Le Monde*, 13 February 2009, 'Un reportage sur les "békés" enflamme la Martinique'. http://www.lemonde.fr/politique/article/2009/02/13/un-reportage-sur-les-bekes-enflamme-la-martinique_1154769_823448.html, consulted 3 August 2013, 6pm.

37 Beckles, 'White Women and Slavery', 67.

Community in 'Global' Academies: The Critical Positioning of 'Meta-Francophone' Caribbeanists

MARY GALLAGHER

Abstract:

Caribbeanists working on the Francophone Caribbean within the Anglophone academy are perhaps particularly well placed to bring into focus the linguistic and cultural losses of the dislocations and relocations of High Capitalism. Although our object of study should facilitate critical insights into the fundamental linguistic and cultural indifference and irresponsibility of capitalist extraction models and into what is at stake politically and ethically in contemporary versions of those profiteering models, the commercialist reductionism currently (re-)formatting not just our own pulverized academic universe, but the entire globe over which it has by now comprehensively spread, surely works against any such truly critical positioning.

Keywords: French/Francophone, English/Globish, Caribbeanists, global academy, globalization, community, responsibility

This study reflects on the rather open and nebulous academic community associated with a specific object of study: the culture of the Francophone Caribbean (Guadeloupe, Martinique and Haiti), a culture forged through the stresses and strains of global displacement. This putative academic community is, like all communities, axiomatically unconstructed or 'inoperable' as Jean-Luc Nancy puts it.[1] If not a community of academic labour, it is at least a community of (mutual) reference or citation. However, unlike the academic community centred on more Franco-French areas of scholarship, such as Renaissance poetry or the eighteenth-century epistolary novel, for example, it appears to be located principally in the Anglo-American

Paragraph 37.2 (2014): 290–307
DOI: 10.3366/para.2014.0127
© Edinburgh University Press
www.euppublishing.com/para

academy. Indeed, its location raises a number of important questions concerning contemporary academic globalization, a phenomenon driven largely by the Anglo-American academy.

With corporate universities increasingly advertising their competitive global reach and impact, what is the ethical and political position of the academic community working on the Francophone Caribbean from or within an institutional position not just outside the Francophone Caribbean but outside the Francophone world in general? How does the work of this community relate both to the local and to the global scale of contemporary academic operations? These are the central questions that will be addressed in this article, although they imply many other issues that would each merit more detailed attention than they can receive here. For example, who, apart from one another, are the readers for whom these academics write, and for whom their labours are of value? To whom is this academic work responsible and how responsible is it? To what extent does its institutional context and/or the language in which it is written and received matter? How local and global, how transnational and translingual is the Francophone Caribbean cultural work driving this scholarship? How subject to non-transmission or to misreading? And finally, how and where does this cultural production and indeed the academic work based upon it acquire exchange value, and for whom?

The postcolonial fallout of three centuries of European expansionism is commonly viewed as the principal, although not the sole, historical factor of the putatively worldwide connectivity that we like to call globalization, a hyper-capitalist 'mobilization' that seems to recuperate all contemporary cultural production and its critical reception. However located or dislocated, unified or fragmented they might be, and wherever they are situated, most Francophone communities located outside Europe have indeed emerged through the expansionary (mass-)migration of traders and colonists. Yet it is not just this intransitive migration, but also the transitive mass-trafficking or mass-transportation — of traded Africans in particular — that is at the heart of the Caribbean differential equation. In other words, the position of the Caribbean at the epicentre of the European slave trade distinguishes the globalized ethos of this particular cultural space from that of other Francophone spaces outside Europe, in Africa or Canada, for example. This history is, moreover, the source of the exceptionally favourable academic head start and tailwinds that the 'Other America' taken as a whole — and thereby Caribbeanists — have enjoyed for almost half a century in relation to the contemporary episteme.[2]

For, whether we call it post-colonialism, transnationalism, migrancy or globalization, that episteme is centred on a critical confrontation with the intersection of extraction capitalism, on the one hand, and unprecedented levels of mobility or migration, on the other. Nowhere and never, however, has that intersection been as dramatic as in the uniquely dehumanizing configuration of the 'New World' plantation system. Moreover, this system was nowhere as concentrated, or indeed as concentrationary, as in the diminutive islands of the Caribbean archipelago.

It is not difficult to understand, then, the fascination that the Caribbean holds in the context of the contemporary episteme, which is so firmly based on globalization. Scholars of globalization naturally look to the multiple Caribbean crucibles to examine, for example, to what extent migratory or diasporic origins programme lasting trans-identitarian proclivities or extra-territorial gravitations. And they often find that a history of dislocation and re-location is indeed associated with a strongly centrifugal memorial tropism right across the Americas. However, in the Caribbean in particular, because of the significant difficulties involved in leaving an island, this history can also give rise to a compensatory preoccupation with adventitious rooting and dwelling. The cut-off, fragmented space of the individual Caribbean islands is mimicked and reinforced in the autarchic configuration of the plantation and in the linguistic diversity and discontinuity of the space as a whole, where islands of French are located beside islands of English or of Spanish.[3] In other words, the Caribbean is distinguished, even in relation to the rest of the 'Other America', by the fact that, in this space, consciousness of a *general* non-aboriginal but nonetheless inaugural intercontinental cut and of its legacy of disruption and discontinuity is supplemented by the extreme geographical, cultural and linguistic disjunction and discontinuity informing this splintered archipelagic space.

The spatial isolation of islands — small islands in particular — has always perhaps acted, independently of, or in tandem with, forces of colonialism and imperialism, as an impetus to dis-identification. This is no doubt in part why Irish writers like Joyce and Beckett, for example, were impelled by exit strategies that were neither fully euphoric nor fully dysphoric, and that were not necessarily, and often not in the slightest, magnetized by colonial (metro)poles. In the Caribbean as also in Ireland, two sets of forces were superimposed: firstly, the persistently unsettling *Unheimlichkeit* caused by the historically coercive deculturation associated with colonial (trans)plantation, dispossession and alienation; and secondly the cabin-fever induced by living in a linguistically dislocated or cut-off space, whether balkanized or archipelagic or not, on small if not tiny islands. The depth of the cultural fascination exerted on writers and thinkers by the uniquely — geologically and culturally — fractured yet recombinant space of the colonized Caribbean was considerably reinforced by the fact that the tiny Antilles — Guadeloupe, St Lucia and Trinidad — gave the world three Literature Nobel laureates, and more generally, literary work that brings to a head all the complex questions regarding the aesthetic, cultural, ethical and political stakes of world-scale cultural mobility and diversity. Almost axiomatically, contemporary Caribbean writing is imbricated in stories of an almost incomparably complicated story of 'inoperable' community, and of exponentially difficult, disrupted dwelling.

The efferent or unsettled gravitations of Caribbean culture are evident in the fact that the very notion of 'écriture migrante' was developed from within French-speaking Canada, in response to the vital presence within this North American space of immigrant French-speaking authors from the 'Other American' South, most notably Haitians, writing there in French. In a less dynamic or less mobile vein, the poetics of 'Relation' or of the 'Tout-Monde' are the more allusive and specular terms in which the Martinican author Édouard Glissant envisions the extreme interconnectivity of the contemporary world(-wide) order. These world-scale or global 'envisionings' were foreshadowed, however, in the 1960s by Glissant's much more locally inflected metadiscourse on the highly problematic differential equation of Caribbean cultural community. His 'Discours antillais' (Caribbean discourse) situated 'antillanité' (or 'Caribbeanness') on a geo-cultural or geo-political level and also, on a more cultural level, in relation to the phenomenon of 'créolisation'. This latter term refers to the creative and recombinant indigenization of culture consequent on displacement.[4] In fact, Glissant's diagnosis of the extreme discontinuity and interconnectivity, diversity and disruption of Caribbean culture was rapidly reconfigured by Glissant himself as a prophetic paradigm of globalization, writ large. Globalized *avant la lettre*, the Caribbean crucible had an early start, then, in encouraging thinkers to reflect upon the ways in which the competing imperatives of poetics, ethics and politics can play out in relation not just to a story of mass colonial and post-colonial migration, whether voluntary or coerced, but also in relation to situations of polyglossia and of unrestrained extraction capitalism.

The question of a cultural community based on creolization, rather than on disjunctive identities, is one of the principal openings explored not just in Caribbean writing, but in all writing from the 'Other America'. For Glissant, indeed, the entire alter-American corpus articulates the 'roman *du nous*' (novel *of the we*)[5] where the 'nous' is a discursive rather than a disjunctive reference. Glissant also argues that all contemporary discourse takes place within the poetics of 'relation' defining the 'Tout-Monde'.[6] This implicit integration of the separate or the specific within the communal, of the 'Je' within the 'nous', suggests here an apparent indifference to the immanence that Rilke called the 'infinite solitude' of the Work (of art).[7] This indifference does, of course raise some deep questions regarding the aesthetics/politics relation, questions that lie for the most part, however, beyond the scope of this study.

One crucial aspect of this apparent indifference must be addressed here, however. It concerns the distinctness of discrete languages and the value of that particular separateness. For exogenous writers like Lafcadio Hearn or James Clifford, Jean-Paul Sartre, André Breton or Paul Morand, the Caribbean crucible is in its very principle (that is, in theory, overall or globally) an intellectually magnetic object of study because of its cultural palimpsest, its cultural creolization. There is, of course, something fundamentally generic about this Caribbean 'principle' of *métissage* and creolization: it does indeed transcend differences of geographical scale as well as linguistic differences. For contemporary scholars too, it is the general theory, the overarching principle, or the global vision of Caribbean dislocation and impaction that is compelling as an early model of globalization provided by this Early Modern laboratory of displacement. Indeed, both exogenous and endogenous commentators are much more interested in the general principle than in the various texts or distinct languages in which this or that singular 'Caribbean discourse' plays out in a specific tongue.

The academic community that takes the linguistically isolated, minority splinters of the Francophone Caribbean as its object of study is, as already mentioned, predominantly 'exogenous' in that it is associated primarily with the Anglo-American academy. This community could be said, then, to dwell on, or to live off, displacement, in at least four crucial ways. Firstly, we are translating a culture that is not ours, either linguistically or geo-politically. Secondly, we are mediating work that emanates from an impacted history — or 'their-story' — of extreme spatial, temporal, cultural and linguistic dislocation. Thirdly, we are, as a consequence of the first two factors, particularly at home in, or at least particularly engaged with, the paradigm of displacement that is credited with predominating in this neo-global age. It was James Clifford who, somewhat problematically, proclaimed in 1988 in *The Predicament of Culture*, not only that we (human beings in general?) are 'all Caribbeans now living in our urban archipelagos', but also that we are all 'dwelling in travel',[8] just as Salman Rushdie explained that we are 'all translated beings living in translated worlds'.[9] Fourthly, most prominent Francophone Caribbeanists, whether they write in French or in English, are working from and for institutions occupying positions of academic and discursive, but above all, competitive trading hegemony within the almost axiomatically Globish-speaking 'knowledge economy'. The value of their work is located in the first instance in relation to the Anglo-Global Higher Education stock exchange.

On the global Higher Education stock exchange, however (and this is the crux of the matter), the French language is not a bullish value. Even in French academia, which is increasingly being realigned along global Higher Education market values, its stock has been falling for some time. One symptom of this devaluation is the pressure being exerted on French academics working in many 'grandes écoles' or universities, both in the humanities and in the sciences, to teach their subject not in their native French but rather in English (or Globish) to classes populated both by local and international students. Another is the series of changes of institutional address of 'Franco-Caribbean studies' within the Anglo academy, a series of shifts which all reflect the ever-strengthening grip of academic globalization. This trend has thus seen academics move institutional home from departments of *French* to departments of *French Studies* and thence to departments of *Francophone (or French and Francophone) Studies*. This change of address can be explained by the felt imperialism and anachronism of the term 'French' as a singular qualifier (specifying a discipline, for example, as in a 'department of French (Studies)'), and by its perceived restrictiveness to a circumscribed European, metropolitan space. As for the academy in France, the erstwhile academic marginalization or even ghettoization of 'Francophone' culture or literature has been dramatically reversed over a relatively short space of time. The reversal is widely recognized today as France's best hope for playing catch-up in the globalization game.[10]

The perceptible shifts of emphasis from French to English within the French academy and from French to Francophone within the Anglo academy have coincided with other displacements, particularly widespread in the Anglo-American academy. For example, the translation of French and/or Francophone Studies — along with Area Studies in general — into Cultural Studies. Or more widely still, and perhaps more significantly, the cancellation of the autonomy of erstwhile units of 'French and/or Francophone Studies' — an autonomy based on a specific focus on *French*. This autonomy was widely ceded as the discipline was absorbed into the more mobile and generic spaces — 'non-lieux' (non-places), perhaps, rather more than 'lieux communs' (common places)[11] — of Schools of Languages (and Literatures), Schools of Comparative Literature, Schools of (Inter-)Cultural Studies, of Translation Studies, of Post-colonial Studies, and so on. These more multi- or interdisciplinary structures might appear to translate a move towards a wider community based on greater intercultural and interlinguistic mobility and connectivity. Unfortunately, however, the genericization associated with this new emphasis on 'translational mobility' has sometimes had a less than positive effect on the standards and concentration of undergraduate studies in specific 'target' languages and cultures. It has certainly not raised the stock of French *either* as an academic language of study *or* as an academic subject in itself. Moreover, it has rarely strengthened the solidity and solidarity of the wider franco-centric meta-community, producing instead a rather attenuated sense of shared responsibility for French/Francophone studies. Moreover, there is a sizeable, associated risk that the contemporary contraction of the wider meta-community of scholars focused on the study and teaching of all that French can be and of all that (world-wide) cultural expression in French can be, will be further exacerbated by the fact that the rate of cross-linguistic Globish/French exchange in 'Franco-Caribbean' research is extraordinarily low.

As noted at the outset of this article, the contemporary Haitian, Martinican or Guadelopean academy is not itself the primary site of Franco-Caribbeanist academic discourse. Moreover, the metro-politan French academy itself has not been in the vanguard of this discourse either. Indeed, apart from a handful of critics such as Dominique Chancé, Dominique Combe or Romuald Fonkoua (to cite only three), very few French or Francophone academics working *within the French or Francophone academy* are widely referenced in Anglophone studies of the Francophone Caribbean. Very many renowned French/Francophone scholars working on the Francophone Caribbean — Lydie Moudiléno, Madeleine Cottenet-Hage, Bernadette Cailler, Valérie Loichot, Mireille Rosello or

Françoise Lionnet, for example — are all based outside the French/Francophone academy. As the 'Pour une littérature du tout-monde en français' debate in France made clear — from 2007 — metropolitan French critical discourse was somewhat slow to adopt the globalization paradigm.[12] In comparison, the Anglo academy has shown for some considerable time immense interest in the French Caribbean. The universities of Liverpool, Birmingham and Nottingham house nerve-cells of Francophone Caribbean scholarship, as do several US universities like the University of Virginia and Florida State University. The individual Francophone Caribbeanists who write for these presses and for the many prestigious journals in and around this field such as *Small Axe* are scattered right throughout the English-speaking academy, from Ireland to Australia and Canada, and from the UK to the US.

Not surprisingly, the gravitational pull of Francophone Caribbean criticism away from the Franco academy reflects the already mentioned efferent tropisms of Caribbean writing itself. If multi-polar, multi-vectorial and centrifugal cultural forces are axiomatic in the Caribbean basin, what is perhaps most striking about this magnetism is the weakness of the pull towards metropolitan France, and the vastly greater traction exerted by the gravitational field of the Anglophone world and the Anglo academy — often taken, not least by itself — to be synonymous with the global academy. Thus when Gallimard launched the Caribbean cultural manifesto *Éloge de la créolité* in 1989, it quickly brought out a second bilingual edition in both English and French.[13] Moreover, at least three extremely prominent authors from the French Caribbean chose to live and work in the US: the Martinican writer, Édouard Glissant, at Louisiana State University at Baton Rouge and then at the City University of New York (CUNY) Graduate Centre; Maryse Condé, until her recent relocation to Paris, at Columbia; and the Haitian writer Edwidge Danticat has taught creative writing at two US universities in New York and in Miami and writes in the English language (having moved from Haiti to Brooklyn in early adolescence).

The translation flows carrying the work of these three pre-eminent Caribbean authors around the world are quite divergent in the three different cases, just as they were in the case of the Caribbean-born Nobel trinity. The Guadeloupean-born Saint-John Perse spent most of the second half of his life in the US, and like the Martinican Glissant, the Saint-Lucian poet Derek Walcott (Nobel 1992) taught for two decades in the US academy (at the University of Boston). When he retired from there, Walcott took up further academic positions in universities in Canada and the UK, at Alberta and Essex. All of this makes the 2002 Nobel laureate, the Trinidadian novelist V. S. Naipaul, something of an exception, not because he gravitated more towards Britain than the US, but because of his low opinion of the academic world, more particularly of its trade in arts and letters. Predictably, this transcultural mobility has often led to charges of desertion of the local and betrayal of the specific, the national and the political, in favour of the mobility enabled by a world language. Inevitably perhaps, questions of community and home, and of (local) political engagement are asked of migrant writers. The specifics of that mobility or migrancy, more specifically the fact that so many of these writers have migrated into the Anglophone (and not the Francophone) academy, does not seem to be as subject to interrogation or challenge.

The Anglocentric tenor of Francophone Caribbean writing surely has implications for the tenor of the academic community to which mediators or 'passeurs' of the French/Francophone Caribbean belong. This community is essentially responsive; it is, fundamentally, a meta-community and, in that sense, if not parasitical then at least symbiotic. It depends on creative writers and intellectuals producing the material that it interprets and translates. Scholars of the Francophone Caribbean belong, then, to at least three communities: the community of our home institution and the academic culture that it espouses; the dispersed community of writing and reading focused specifically on Caribbean texts written in French; and the 'universal' academic community. As already noted, the academic world that this meta-community of scholarship is writing from or within is predominantly Anglophone. Some of us may write exclusively in French, others exclusively in English, still others in both languages, but if little or none of our work is formally translated into the other language, what does this mean? Does it mean that our work is, to a certain extent, located — not to say locked — within the Anglo academy, and if so, what are the effects of that localization on the meaning and value of what we do? In my experience, critical work on the Francophone Caribbean, when written in English, is not referenced to any appreciable extent by academics or students working in French or in French-speaking institutions, even within the French-speaking Caribbean. An exception to this might be bilingual Canadian academia. The authors of this critical work may regard themselves as writing for the (global) world writ large, including — of course — the French academic world. However, this world is not really receiving them. In reality, unless they are published in French and in France, our efforts do not, in my experience, migrate much across the boundary separating the two academies and the two working languages: French and Anglo-global. As Édouard Glissant wrote in a different context: 'Ils ne savent pas lire le monde' (They don't know how to read the world).[14] To rephrase this, we may earn our academic keep as readers of the Francophone Caribbean, but the French/Francophone world more generally is not much interested or invested, apparently anyway, in what we have to say and, to a lesser extent, the inverse also holds true.

One of the features of this 'apartheid', which even a cursory examination of work in the field confirms, is the very significant investment of Anglophone critical discourse in a certain theoretical, politico-philosophical sophistication, an investment that does not easily cross the linguistic-cultural borders separating the two academies. Taking its cue from, and/or feeding into, both the highly developed theoretical discourse of some of the foremost Francophone Caribbean authors, such as Édouard Glissant and Patrick Chamoiseau, and also the ambient tropisms of the Anglo-American academy, Anglophone critical commentary in the field can seem very focused on a theoretical competitiveness which is stimulating and often exhilarating in its efforts to trump previously articulated theoretical, political or ethical positions. However, this focus is not wholly unproblematic.

Chris Bongie rightly observes in this connexion that, '[w]ith his unflagging advocacy of a creolizing world of Diversity and Relation, Glissant has become one of the few non-hexagonal French-language writers, after Césaire and Fanon, to have made a major impact on postcolonial theory in the Anglo-American academy'.[15] Gratifying as this attention (and vicarious endorsement) may be for the Franco-Caribbean meta-community, the flip-side of the 'impact' of their object of study is the somewhat lesser impression made by 'their' authors in the metropolitan French academy. Furthermore, a less recognized problem sometimes associated with the stated impact is the fact that the work of these authors has not always been responsibly translated in the Anglo-American context. Thus, in a remark on Immanuel Wallerstein's *world systems* theory, Gayatri Chakravorty Spivak references Glissant's thought: 'I consulted the basic texts of the contemporary debate on creolity. Here I will content myself with citing Édouard Glissant, the initiator of the movement.'[16] In fact, Glissant always emphatically distanced himself from the movement in question and from the essentializing concept of *créolité* which

Spivak wants (comparative) literary critics to celebrate:[17] 'If we want to preserve the dignity of that strange adjective "comparative" in comparative literature, we will embrace creolity.'[18]

Several thinkers, including Frederick Cooper and Edward Said, have made a strong case for the need to parse the specificity of the power relations associated with colonialism and imperialism as realized in particular (historical) contexts.[19] Indeed, the author of *Death of a Discipline* is herself a remarkable advocate of the principles of close reading and respectful apprenticeship of, and attention to, both the specific context and the specific language(s) of texts.[20] Yet Spivak's pronouncement on Glissant can be seen as, however unintentionally, edging reading and locale out of the collective (globalized) mind, in favour of less contextualized or embedded, therefore more easily translatable, cultural forms: in this instance, the 'theoretical' shorthand of names, labels, slogans.

When Chris Bongie points out that '[n]o less a luminary than Gayatri Spivak has, for instance, recently stressed her "affinity with Glissant's thinking"' and that this luminary has, more specifically, lauded Glissant's 'vision of "creolity"', the inverted commas encircling 'creolity' could easily appear attributory rather than admonitory. And yet, scare quotes are by no means in short supply in the most critical of Anglophone Caribbeanist commentaries, both on the work of authors from within the Francophone Caribbean itself and on the work of their more soft-focus 'specialist' commentators. For example, Peter Hallward's *Absolutely Postcolonial*[21] and Chris Bongie's *Friends and Enemies* both articulate a certain scepticism regarding the ability or willingness of Caribbean literature's most vaunted champions and/or practitioners to engage adequately with the real political stakes of their discourse and practice.[22] And yet, however compelling these positions may be, they do not obviate the need to make certain more basic points about Caribbeanist meta-discourse and the meta-community configured within the Anglo academy around this meta-discourse.

First of all, the 'creolity' that Gayatri Spivak calls upon all literary scholars to celebrate may be prophetic of the contemporary paradigm of global mobility and translatability, but it is first and foremost a cultural dynamic that is indissociably linked historically to the most nakedly oppressive mode of capitalism ever practised: the New World plantation system. Secondly, while the contemporary work of Caribbeanists may foreground creative resistance to, and cultural subversion of, that oppression, that academic work is itself inscribed in a globally hegemonic neo-liberal model of capital extraction. While this model might not actually wipe out the potentially critical or resistant values either of the cultural production being academically mediated, or of the academic mediation itself, it is as difficult to prevent transmission failures and mistranslations of the cultural resistance being mediated, as it is to prevent the academic work of mediation from itself being measured in relation to anti-academic, anti-intellectual economic proxies such as citation rates, research grants, or student enrolments to exorbitantly priced 'education'.

As several recent critical studies show, resistant forces can be themselves intertwined with, or even embedded within, the very processes that they critique or resist. I am thinking here of studies like Graham Huggan's *The Postcolonial Exotic* or Richard Watts's *Post/Colonial Packaging*.[23] Chris Bongie too makes extensive reference in *Friends and Enemies* to the academic trade in post-colonial literature. Indeed, he has coined the expression 'scribal politics' to refer to the 'relation to and with power in which "literature" as a cultural institution has been entangled since its inception'.[24] When Bongie uses words like 'investment' or 'trading', as in his references to literary critics 'who trade in [this or] that author' or in the title of a chapter on Glissant in his book *Friends and Enemies*, namely 'dealing in relation', he seems to be using the financial discourse metaphorically to describe the currency of critical, epistemological or, as he puts it so well himself, 'scribal' authority. He is aiming, in other words, to underline the compromising 'entanglements' of literary studies with the politics of identity. Because of his concern to expose the political pretensions of literature and of literary critics, it is not completely clear that Chris Bongie includes all of contemporary academia in this particularly problematic ensnarement. Certainly, in his critique of what he regards as the somewhat 'bien pensant' claims for literature or poetics made by Glissant himself in his later work especially, Bongie seems more concerned about some critics' failure to question those claims robustly, than about the 'unfreedom' of most academic critics in respect of their institutional or professional affiliations. Unlike putatively compromising, politically disabling, 'investments' in literature, some very widespread occupational or structural hazards surely also trap academics who profess sociology or politics rather than literature. Indeed, even those who most critically and most knowingly profess Caribbean history or politics rather than Caribbean literature can no doubt turn out to be themselves caught up in the global cash laundering in which Higher Education and academia play such an important role. As such they are surely implicated both in the overheating academic research industry that operates at times in almost complete dereliction of certain educational responsibilities and in an unrestrained Higher Education market relentlessly capitalized upon (*cui bono?*) through the sales machinery of credit ratings and league tables.

Thus, Chris Bongie's reference to what he calls the 'generalized tendency in (Francophone) postcolonial studies to avoid any full reckoning with the scribal dimension of literature, its institutional status and the strategies of legitimization through which it perpetuates itself' might leave us relatively sanguine.[25] Given the acuity of critical insight of Caribbeanist critics such as Bongie himself and of so many of the others cited or not in *Friends and Enemies*, including Celia Britton, Nick Nesbitt, Peter Hallward, Elizabeth DeLoughrey and Françoise Lionnet to name just five — not to mention all those Caribbeanists working in French outside, or at least at an angle to, the French and Francophone academy — one would have to be positive about the standard of the critical reflection not just of the 'scribal dimension of [Francophone Caribbean] literature', but of the 'institutional status' of that literature both within and beyond the Anglophone academy.

Unfortunately, however, it is less easy to be sanguine about the ability or inability of academic communities in general to protect both the value of linguistic diversity in and for itself, and also the existential and ethical, political and aesthetic value of linguistic or cultural work (or play) which points beyond the economy of knowledge or the knowledge economy. Although the main point of the work of the dispersed Anglophone meta-community centred on the Francophone Caribbean might be to try to read the latter for and with our students and our more remote readers, our prima facie responsibility as educators is surely as readers and as translators of *French-language* culture. As such we are answerable above all to language and to languages, as well as to the work of those individuals and communities who live and think in those languages.

In that sense, unless we believe that Caribbeanist metadiscourse lies outside the spurious spin of contemporary academic commodification and extraction capitalism, the critique of the marketing of individual 'authors' or 'areas' or 'cultural communities' should perhaps be extended to the marketing of our own academic practice. That would mean making the critical connexion between the institutions for which we work and which capitalize on our work, on the one hand, and, on the other hand, what those institutions may be doing to linguistically deep and detailed critical thought, and thereby to language and especially to linguistic diversity, all in the name of business strategies based *in fine* on growth and profit.

If globalization is the new imperialism and if Globish is its medium, then is our work still inscribed in community or communities or just in a single market? If the latter, then is this market truly 'free' or just 'unrestrained'? Is it truly open onto the entire globe or uncritically 'Globish'? To which ends is our work being subordinated, instrumentalized, exploited? What, in other words, is its real or full impact? Not, then, the impact as assessed by the 'Research Excellence Framework', but in terms of its defence or undermining of communities of language or culture? If one obvious problem of the contemporary academy is the suffocation or 'disappearing' of non-Globish languages or formats, and if another equally serious threat is the deep and detailed study of 'other' languages (because this apprenticeship demands so much — very — costly time and effort), then perhaps the underlying issue that needs to be confronted is the less grandiose than fear-induced, linguicidal ambition of academic corporations transfixed by the their global standing.

The value of global mobility has been central to the rise of that sometimes malignant off-shoot of globalization, globalized academic capitalism, the relentless promotion of which has been demonstrably hostile to linguistic diversity and discrimination. Coincidentally, academic internationalization and globalization have also been destructive, in certain cases at least, of intrinsic academic values such as critical freedom, independence and responsibility. In some contexts, for example, global academic capitalism can be shown to have managed — via the creeping casualization of academic labour and through the unilateral alteration of certain contractual terms even of tenured employment — to distance academics from at least one of the traditionally unquestioned values and norms of the international academic community, namely 'academic freedom', making them subject not to those widely agreed norms, but rather to the specific aims, targets, goals and objectives of their particular corporate employer. In certain cases, this reform has merely copper-fastened the forced alignment of academic productivity and performance on lucrative student recruitment targets and the attraction of maximal research funding income. In this author's experience, the forces of contemporary globalization have transformed the university from a (very far, of course, from unproblematic) space of what would be termed 'Bildung' in German, acculturation in English or 'formation' in French, into a space of Globish formatting, of managerial and administrative conformity and uniformity, and from a locally or nationally invested politics of cultural capitalism to a transnational, post-political empire of technocratic administration.[26] This development coincided, again in certain instances at least, with the consolidation of what one could only call 'linguicidal', but also 'theoritarian', trends. Some concrete examples of the former would include: the merging of distinct language departments into new umbrella cost centres called Schools of Languages and Cultures, or Schools of Languages and Literatures, a shift that often coincides with other moves: the termination of various 'non-viable' language units: Arabic, Hebrew, Italian, Russian, German. . .; the cutting of academic posts, even despite buoyant student enrolments, by as much as two thirds; the inauguration of quixotic undergraduate degree programmes 'covering' two or even three of the surviving languages/literatures; and the concomitant resource-sparing and cost-cutting development of generic survey courses, delivered exclusively in English and advertised as 'interdisciplinary': firm favourites would be 'Critical Theory', 'Cultural Theory', or 'Post-Colonial Theory'. The consequences of all of these developments for educational standards in the teaching of 'languages' and 'texts' are, inevitably, inestimable.

As the dispersed meta-community of Anglophone scholars of the Francophone Caribbean attempts to translate the aesthetic, ethical and political resonance of writing from and around the Francophone Caribbean, should we simply ignore the *inscription of our own work* in the overheating empire of academic capital? Should we block out or deny the ways in which that resonance, and/or our mediation of it, either does or does not travel, either is or is not transmitted, received or translated? Should we be bothered by the implications of our own entrapment in the 'repeating island' of an ever more closed, monolingual academy? Should we be concerned that some of us are (still) being coerced, despite the progress and insights of World Literature Studies or Translation Studies, into teaching texts in translation as though they could have been written in any (other) language, or into teaching theory as though thought can be communicated independently of discourse, text and context? Should we be accepting, as some of us (still) are, our institutions' disinvestments from language scholarship in favour of bland, but infinitely cheaper, 'content' courses? Just as importantly, perhaps, should we be concerned about the ways in which our work is instrumentalized, measured, entered in what is essentially a closed and controlled competition with that of our colleagues, immediate or distant? If we should, how might we resist, labouring as we do in our separate institutions, jurisdictions and worlds, in our disjunctive 'repeating islands', the ways in which our critical thinking is being neutralized by its commodification and by its ever more exorbitantly priced promotion and sale to students? Finally, how could we challenge the ways in which these sales are then fed into the global or national university rankings that in turn determine university funding in a perfect neo-liberal circle?

Caribbeanists working on the Francophone Caribbean within the Anglophone academy are perhaps particularly well placed to bring into focus the high ethical and political stakes, but also the linguistic and cultural costs and consequences of the dislocations and relocations of High Capitalism. We are particularly well placed to develop insights into the fundamental linguistic and cultural indifference of capitalist extraction models and into what is at stake in contemporary versions of those models and of that indifference. There may well exist, therefore, within both the local and the global academic communities to which Caribbeanists belong, especially Anglophone scholars of the Francophone Caribbean, an unspoken alignment, commonality or even consensus of critical resistance towards some of the commercialist reductionism currently dominating not just their own academic universe, but the entire globe over which it has by now comprehensively spread. If so, that resistance is not easily registered, and even when it is, is instantly converted into the very currency being resisted. As a result, it can be difficult, in our 'privileged' discipline at least, to avoid experiencing the question of academic community as — at best — a question of (to quote Nick Nesbitt) becoming 'free in understanding our own immersion in unfreedom'.[27]

NOTES

1 Jean-Luc Nancy argues that community is not the result of a process, project or programme of production, whether cultural, social, economic or political. It cannot be pre-scribed or planned into existence. See *La Communauté désœuvrée* (Paris: Christian Bourgois, 1986); *The Inoperative Community*, edited by Peter Connor, translated by Peter Connor, Lisa Garbus, Michael Holland and Simona Sawhney, with a foreword by Christopher Fynsk (Minneapolis: Minnesota University Press, 1991).

2 In *Le Discours antillais* (Paris: Seuil, 1981), 256, in a chapter entitled 'Le Roman des Amériques', Glissant admits in a footnote that his text concerns essentially 'l'Autre Amérique (Antilles et Amérique du Sud)' (the other

America: the Antilles and South America). 'The Other America' was the title of an important book on poverty in the US (Michael Harrington, *The Other America* (New York: Macmillan, 1962)), but the sense given to the expression by Glissant in order to distinguish this part of the Americas from the more industrialized, urban North, was taken up by J. Michael Dash in *The Other America: Literature in a New World Context* (Charlottesville: University of Virginia Press, 1998). J. Michael Dash's translation of certain sections of Glissant's 1981 work was published as Édouard Glissant, *Caribbean Discourse: Selected Essays* (Charlottesville: Virginia University Press, 1989).

3   See Antonio Benitez-Rojo, *The Repeating Island: The Caribbean and the Postmodern Perspective*, translated by J. Maraniss (Durham, NC: Duke University Press, 1992).

4   Some of Glissant's metadiscourse in *Le Discours antillais* was adumbrated in the late 1950s and 1960s in the essays published in his *Soleil de la conscience* (Paris: Seuil, 1956) and *L'Intention poétique* (Paris: Seuil, 1969).

5   *Le Discours antillais*, 153.

6   See especially Édouard Glissant, *Poétique de la relation* and *Traité du Tout-Monde* (Paris: Gallimard, 1997).

7   Letter 3 (23 April 1903): 'works of art are of an infinite solitude and no means of approach is so useless as criticism.' Rainer Maria Rilke, *Letters to a Young Poet*, translated by M. D. Herter Norton (New York: W. W. Norton & Co., 1993).

8   James Clifford, *The Predicament of Culture: Twentieth-Century Ethnography, Literature and Art* (Cambridge, MA: Harvard University Press, 1988), 173; James Clifford, *Routes: Travel and Translation in the Late Twentieth Century* (Cambridge, MA: Harvard University Press, 1997), 2.

9   Salman Rushdie, *Imaginary Homelands: Essays and Criticism 1981–91* (London: Granta, 1991), 13.

10   For a careful study of the evolution of the French/Francophone academy in respect of postcolonial studies and for a real attempt to situate the two academies in relation to each other, see *Francophone Postcolonial Studies: A Critical Introduction*, edited by Charles Forsdick and David Murphy (London: Arnold, 2003).

11   I am using the expression 'lieu commun' in its literal meaning of 'shared space'. Both the 'lieu commun' and the 'non-lieu' are shared spaces with an attenuated specificity based in part on their non-appropriation and/or non-specification. However, unlike the somewhat specific disposition implied by the intersections characterizing the 'lieu commun' (Jean-Luc Nancy thus defines a given 'world' as the 'lieu commun d'un ensemble de lieux' (common ground of a set of places), Jean-Luc Nancy, *La Création du monde ou la mondialisation* (Paris: Galilée, 2002), 36), the 'non-lieu', as conceived by Marc Augé (in *Non-Lieux: introduction à une anthropologie de la surmodernité*

(Paris: Seuil, 1992)), is so completely unspecified as to be non-conducive to any of the intersections, and certainly to any of the shared identifications and responsibilities on which community is based.

12 See Dominique Combe, *Les Littératures francophones: questions, débats, polémiques* (Paris: Presses universitaires de France, 2010); and 'Littératures francophones, littérature-monde en français', *Modern and Contemporary France* 18:2 (2010), 231–49.

13 Jean Bernabé, Patrick Chamoiseau, and Raphaël Confiant, *Eloge de la créolité* (Paris: Gallimard, 1989).

14 *Traité du Tout-Monde*, 242.

15 Chris Bongie, *Friends and Enemies: The Scribal Politics of Post/Colonial Literature* (Liverpool: Liverpool University Press, 2010), 331.

16 Gayatri Chakravorty Spivak, 'World Systems and the Creole', *Narrative* 14:7 (2007), 102–12 (109).

17 Further examples of this kind of 'transmission failure' of the Francophone Caribbean are studied in Mary Gallagher, 'Connection Failures: Discourse on Contemporary European and Caribbean Writing', *Small Axe* 14:3 (2010), 21–32. For an account of some of the criticism directed at the *créolité* movement, see Mary Gallagher, 'The *Créolité* Movement: Paradoxes of a French Caribbean Orthodoxy' in *Creolization: History, Ethnography, Theory*, edited by Charles Stewart (Walnut Creek, CA: Left Coast, 2007), 220–37.

18 G. C. Spivak, 'World Systems and the Creole', 110.

19 See Frederick Cooper, *Colonialism in Question: Theory, Knowledge, History* (Berkeley: University of California Press, 2005); and Edward Said, *Culture and Imperialism* (New York: Vintage, 1994).

20 G. C. Spivak, *Death of a Discipline* (New York: Columbia University Press, 2003). The discipline referred to in the title is that of unreconstructed Comparative Literature Studies.

21 Peter Hallward, *Absolutely Postcolonial: Writing between the Singular and the Specific* (Manchester: Manchester University Press, 2010).

22 This critique is contested by Celia Britton in 'Globalization and Political Action in the Work of Edouard Glissant', *Small Axe* 13 (2009), 1–11.

23 Graham Huggan, *The Postcolonial Exotic: Marketing the Margins* (London: Routledge, 2001); Richard Watts, *Packaging Post/Coloniality: The Manufacture of Literary Identity in the Francophone World* (Lanham, MD: Lexington, 2005).

24 Bongie, *Friends and Enemies*, 133.

25 Bongie, *Friends and Enemies*, 142.

26 See Bill Readings, *The University in Ruins* (Cambridge, MA: Harvard University Press, 1996), one of the first critical studies of this transformation.

27 Nick Nesbitt, *Voicing Memory: History and Subjectivity in French Caribbean Literature* (Charlotteville: University of Virginia Press, 2003), 40.

Notes on Contributors

Charles Forsdick is James Barrow Professor of French at the University of Liverpool, and UK Arts and Humanities Research Council Theme Leadership Fellow for 'Translating Cultures'. He has published widely on travel writing, colonial history and postcolonial literatures. He is also a specialist on Haiti and the Haitian Revolution, and has written on representations of Toussaint Louverture. His publications include *Victor Segalen and the Aesthetics of Diversity* (Oxford University Press, 2000) and *Travel in Twentieth-Century French and Francophone Cultures* (Oxford University Press, 2005).

Mary Gallagher teaches French and Francophone Studies at University College Dublin. She has published on Caribbean writing — *La Créolité de Saint-John Perse* (Gallimard, 1998) and *Soundings in French Caribbean Writing since 1950* (OUP, 2002) — and on postcolonial positionings more generally: *World Writing: Poetics, Ethics, Globalization* (University of Toronto Press, 2008). She is also the author of *Academic Armageddon: an Irish Requiem for Higher Education* (Liffey Press, 2012), and is completing a study of Lafcadio Hearn's Creole trajectory.

Mairéad Hanrahan is Professor of French at University College London. She has written widely on the work of Jean Genet, including *Lire Genet: Une Poétique de la différence* (1997) and an edited collection, *Genet* (2004). She has also edited volumes on *Literature and the Mathematical* (2007), and *Cixous, Derrida, Psychoanalysis* (2013), and her monograph *Cixous's Semi-Fictions: Thinking At the Borders of Fiction* will appear with Edinburgh University Press in September 2014. She is a member of the Editorial Board of *Paragraph*.

Kate Hodgson is currently a British Academy Postdoctoral Research Fellow at the University of Liverpool. Her research focuses on Haiti and the nineteenth-century politics of anti-slavery. She completed a Ph.D on the afterlives of the Haitian Revolution in 2010 at UCL, supervised by Celia Britton. She is the co-editor of two collections,

Paragraph 37.2 (2014): 308–310
DOI: 10.3366/para.2014.0128
© Edinburgh University Press
www.euppublishing.com/para

Slavery, Memory and Identity (Pickering and Chatto, 2012) and *Between Memory and Forgetting: Commemorating Slavery in the Francophone World* (Liverpool University Press, forthcoming 2015). She has also published on Haiti and state memorialization, abolitionist travellers in the Caribbean, and the politics of anti-slavery.

Maeve McCusker is Senior Lecturer in French at Queen's University Belfast. She has published widely on Antillean writing, notably *Patrick Chamoiseau: Recovering Memory* (Liverpool University Press, 2007), and a scholarly edition of one of the first Martinican novels, Louis de Maynard's *Outre-mer* (L'Harmattan, 2009 [1835]). She has recently co-edited two collections of essays: *The Conte. Oral and Written Dynamics* (Lang, 2010) and *Islanded Identities. Constructions of Postcolonial Cultural Insularity* (Rodopi, 2011), and is currently writing a book on the construction of whiteness in Antillean writing.

Lorna Milne is Professor of French and Vice-Principal (Proctor) at St Andrews University, where she was Dean of Arts 2006–09. Her research interests include the modern and contemporary novel in French, especially Antillean literature. She has published monographs on Michel Tournier and Patrick Chamoiseau as well as articles and edited volumes on French literature and politics.

Martin Munro is Winthrop-King Professor of French and Francophone Studies at Florida State University. He previously worked in Scotland, Ireland and Trinidad. His recent publications include: *American Creoles: The Francophone Caribbean and the American South* (Liverpool, 2012); *Different Drummers: Rhythm and Race in the Americas* (California, 2010); *Edwidge Danticat: A Reader's Guide* (Virginia, 2010); and *Haiti Rising: Haitian History, Culture, and the Earthquake of 2010* (Liverpool/UWI, 2010). His latest book is *Writing on the Fault Line: Haitian Literature and the Earthquake of 2010* (Liverpool, forthcoming 2014). He is currently working on the theme of the apocalypse in the Caribbean. He is Director of the Winthrop-King Institute for Contemporary French and Francophone Studies at Florida State University.

Eva Sansavior is Lecturer in French at the University of Limerick, Ireland. Her research centres on representations of 'the political' and 'the aesthetic' in French and Francophone postcolonial literary and visual cultures. She is author of *Maryse Condé and the Space of Literature* (Oxford: Legenda, 2012) and co-editor (with Richard Scholar) of *Caribbean Globalizations: 1492 to the Present Day* (Liverpool University Press, forthcoming).

Eli Park Sorensen is an assistant professor in the College of Liberal Studies at Seoul National University (South Korea), specializing in postcolonial studies, comparative literature, and cultural studies. He received his Ph.D in Comparative Literature from University College London in 2007. He has published the book *Postcolonial Studies and the Literary* with Palgrave Macmillan (2010).

Michael Syrotinski is Marshall Professor of French at Glasgow University. He has published widely on Francophone African literature and contemporary theory. His publications include *Singular Performances* (Virginia UP, 2002), *Deconstruction and the Postcolonial* (Liverpool UP, 2007), and an edited special issue of *The Senses and Society* (2013) on the work of Jean-Luc Nancy. He is a member of the Editorial Board of *Paragraph*.